CW00543387

CORDON ROUGE

VEGETARIAN AND VEGAN RECIPES
FROM THE RED HERRING

To all workers, past, present and future

Earthright Publications
Red Herring Workers' Co-operative

British Cataloguing in Publication Data available

© Red Herring Workers' Co-operative Ltd 1996
Reprinted 1998

Co-published by

Earthright Publications
8 Ivy Avenue
Ryton, Tyne and Wear
NE40 3PU

ISBN 0 907367 10 0

and

Red Herring Workers' Co-operative Ltd
4 Studley Terrace
Newcastle upon Tyne
NE4 5AH

ISBN 0 9516622 1 X

Typeset in Palatino and printed on Reprise recycled paper
at Tyneside Free Press Ltd
5 Charlotte Square
Newcastle upon Tyne
NE1 4XF

Earthright Publications ISBN 0 907367 10 0

Red Herring Workers Co-operative Ltd ISBN 0 9516622 1 X

Contents

Acknowledgements

Monica Frisch for all aspects of book production and being prepared to do another cook book even after, or perhaps because of, her experience with the Red Herring with *Food out of Chile*; Tyneside Free Press for use of their facilities, their invaluable assistance and patience; John Baines for the hand lettering on the cover; John Faulkner for all photographs except where otherwise stated; Mick Sams for the drawings; Eleanor Rogers for the cover illustration, for all her efforts in re-writing and standardising most of the recipes, and for the diagrams for making filo parcels; Nichole Messier for sections on a healthy vegetarian diet, ingredients, tips and techniques, and edible flowers, and for advice and assistance with editing and book production; Mike Toyn for getting the text sections into some sort of order and for soliciting contributions from former Co-op members; Nigel Wild for information on the history of the Red Herring, on how to bake bread, and for having the idea; Jenny Jones for the cake section and 'Bake to Basics'; Steve Ridd for the book launch and publicity; Adele Sherif for the book launch, publicity and the fish motif; Jo Ackerman, with assistance from our loyal casual staff, for keeping the Red Herring going whilst everyone else was preoccupied with the book; all those former Co-op members who sent in contributions; Jon Nott for advice and assistance with design and artwork; and finally, all our friends and partners for support and patience.

Foreword

Some months back we Herrings realised that the cafe was approaching its tenth birthday. Apart from feeling amazed, we wanted to mark it somehow. It was suggested we produce a cookbook. As customers have frequently urged us to do one, this seemed the perfect occasion. A little history, some anecdotes and images would combine with favourite recipes to make a cookbook with a little more!

Throughout this book are short passages about the history, roots and significant events of the past ten years of the Red Herring. They cover the period from the original anarchic Red Herring being opened, through to the bakery being built, becoming a co-operative, the return to Chile of founder members Victor and Maria, and Nigel's visit to Durham at Her Majesty's pleasure.

For much of the early period Nigel was the sole proprietor of the Red Herring. As our only remaining founding member his perspective makes him uniquely qualified to write about us. Yet there have been many who have contributed to the Red Herring in various ways over the years. Many have been Co-op members, and we've tried to include some of their voices here, too. Others, too numerous to mention, have helped to flavour the place and keep it going. We thank them all, as well as the friends still to come. The Red Herring has become its own creature, and is more than merely the sum of all its parts. May we all continue to enjoy it for many years to come!

The Red Herring, September 1996

Sally Brown's beautiful fish map poster to re-launch the Red Herring as a co-operative in 1988 (much used since in many forms).

Vegetarian Cookery at the Red Herring

Since it first opened ten years ago, the Red Herring has been serving high quality vegetarian food to nourish the soul and conscience as much as the body. In this last decade vegetarianism has grown in popularity. Many pubs and restaurants now include vegetarian options on their menus and Newcastle now even has a pub that provides only vegetarian food.

The Red Herring has kept abreast of changing expectations of food, with workers over the years bringing in their own unique, heartfelt concepts of food. Throughout has been the feeling that food nourishes on many levels, aesthetic as well as nutritional and political.

In the initial business plan the Red Herring set out the following aims and objectives. Ten years later, they still form our mandate.

The aims of the Red Herring are:

1. To provide an honest living in a pleasant environment providing food and services without exploitation of animals, workers, customers or suppliers, however distant from us.

2. To expand and develop the idea of working together to provide for our needs.

3. To provide good, unadulterated food without additives or preservatives and to use organically produced ingredients where possible.

4. To provide an outside catering service and develop our abilities to do this.

5. To be aware of our effect on the environment with what we do to minimise waste; to recycle and to compost where possible.

6. To monitor and improve our practices of work including health and hygiene; to develop and share our knowledge and skills in all its aspects.

7. To provide help and facilities for cultural and culinary exchanges.

Early morning bakers: Steve rolling out croissant dough and Nigel putting a pizza base on a tray.

Jenny taking a sharp left hander on her way to the shop with the barrow of bread and goodies for 10 o'clock opening.

A Day in the Life of the Red Herring

Each day there are eight shifts at the Red Herring; each lasts eight hours, so that is 64 hours per day or 320 hours a week that the Co-op works. Each shift is usually worked for a week and people tend to spend more time doing shifts they prefer, are better at and so on, although there is no escaping the nights which are strictly rotated.

The Red Herring day begins at 6 a.m. when two bakers start. They are soon busy making breads, pizza, quiche, croissants and pasties. There is always a bit of a rush as 10 a.m. approaches and the first delivery to the shop is made. Whatever is ready is taken round to the shop on a handcart as near to ten o'clock as possible for when the shop opens.

By 10 a.m. the shop worker will have been busy for three hours; setting out the cafe, filling stotties, stocking shelves and getting baskets ready for the bakers' arrival to put produce in.

The shop worker is not alone in the cafe as at 8 a.m. two cooks arrive and they have to make a soup, starters, salads, main courses, any accompaniments, and sweets. They have two hours until 10 a.m. to work uninterrupted as the cafe doesn't open till then. However at 10 a.m. the 10-6 worker arrives; the 10-6 worker has a support role in the kitchen. They will serve customers with beverages, cakes and croissants, as well as making a green salad and helping as required.

At midday the full menu is available and the kitchen must change roles from food preparation to food serving. There is usually a busy period between 12 and 2, but following this the shop worker and then the cooks have their lunch breaks while the 10-6 worker provides cover. At 2 p.m. the bakers' day ends and they must have left the bakery ready for the next day. At 3 p.m. the shop worker's day ends and the 10-6 worker takes over in the shop until it closes.

The next significant event is when the two evening staff come in at 3.45. There is then 15 minutes until the cooks finish, during which information is exchanged about what is on the menu, how it is served and what is left to do.

At 6 p.m. the first bookings arrive and the cafe takes on the atmosphere of a restaurant. Orders are taken, food is prepared and served and tables are cleared. This continues until 9.45 p.m. which is the deadline for food orders, except sweets. After 10 p.m. the tables are cleared, the kitchen is cleaned and customers begin to leave. Finally the night time staff leave and go home, sometime around midnight.

Activity, 18 hours a day, 5 days a week – the Red Herring hardly sleeps.

A Healthy Vegetarian Diet

Over the years there's been a lot of concern about vegetarians meeting dietary requirements. This has been the cautious approach of a predominantly meat-eating culture, with the idea that meat (and thus protein) was the focus of a complete diet. It is difficult to change the way we were taught it was healthy to eat. If you skip a component, you worry about what's missing.

A healthy diet consists of about 70% complex carbohydrates, 20% protein, and 10% fats.

Widely considered a body fuel, protein is actually there to heal the body's tissues. If you have had an injury, you'll need more protein to heal quickly. The body only uses protein as fuel if there are not enough other sources of energy. The best source of energy is complex carbohydrates, followed by fats as a second choice. Using protein as fuel requires a convoluted process that puts stress on the body. Protein is emergency fuel; in starvation the body uses any incoming protein as an energy source and will even consume its own muscle tissue.

Tofu, tempeh and beans are examples of vegetable-based protein. Beans and seeds are often best supplemented with grains to create the best combinations of amino acids for complete proteins. A bonus of vegetable-based protein is that it is accompanied by little or no saturated fats, whereas animal proteins (including milk and eggs) tend to be high in both saturated fats and cholesterol, which can cause health problems.

The word 'diet' derives from the Greek 'diaita', meaning 'a way of life'.

Vegetarians think of their choice of diet as being more than an elimination of meat. There is an increased awareness of all the multitude of foods they DO eat. Whatever the focus of a meal is, there is an exploration of its nuances. Whole grains, vegetables, fruits and legumes get more attention when they're not just 'side dishes'. Vegetarians expect more of them, in quality, taste, and visual appeal. As a vegetarian, you derive more of your nutrition from them than you used to and your body will digest them easier than it does meat.

Try eating a quarter to half of your food volume raw. This ensures the maximum nutritional benefit for you. Raw foods are low in sodium and contain all their delicate nutrients undamaged by cooking. Eat sprouted beans, seeds and grains for an energy boost. The Red Herring serves most of its food with a variety of colourful salads.

Voluptuous Vegetables

As summer hits its peak and many of our customers go away on holiday, wonderful things happen at the Red Herring that they will not know they've missed. The brief growing season in the North East offers its greatest abundance then, and the Herrings make the most of it. Sweet, tender yellow courgettes, home-grown fresh oregano, damp paperbags of just-picked strawberries and bundles of lemon-spicy lovage are passed from worker to worker as allotments and gardens yield their harvest. Local organic lettuces from the Rising Sun Farm and the North East Organic Growers at Earth Balance make the green salads unparalleled in taste and texture. The lettuce is often cut from the soil within hours of ending up in our salad bowl. At this quietest time of year, the Co-op members savour what the customers miss.

The busiest time is around Christmas. Local leafy greens are less in evidence, except for winter kale, but the menus are planned meticulously to make use of seasonal vegetables. Brussels sprouts are teamed with fragrant chestnuts, roast parsnips and spiced pumpkin pie comfort and warm us as we prepare for Newcastle's long cold nights. And even in the winter, we serve fresh salads.

Vegetables are good for you. They give your body fibre, carbohydrates, vitamins and minerals. Root vegetables generally contain more minerals while leafy greens contain chlorophyll, iron, calcium, vitamin C and vitamin A. Broccoli, cauliflower and cabbage are of the crucifer family and besides containing lots of calcium, are reputedly anti-carcinogenic, as is raw garlic.

Asparagus, broccoli, brussels sprouts, cabbage, sweetcorn, dried beans and peas, and romaine lettuce all contain folic acid. This is an important component in preventing spina bifida, lung cancer and cervical cancer. Folic acid is destroyed by heat, so don't overcook.

Several vegetables contain a substance called oxalic acid, which prevents calcium from being absorbed by your body, and can actually leach it out of you, if you have too much. This seems to be activated after the food containing oxalic acid is cooked. High-oxalic acid foods include spinach, chard and beets. Raw, the oxalic acid doesn't seem to be an issue; and you'd need to consume a lot of it for it to be a problem.

Fruits and vegetables contain much of their nutrients just below their skins. They also store chemical residues from pesticides and fertilisers there. Leaving the skins on maximises the goodness of organic vegetables; they tend to be higher in nutrients than their sprayed counterparts anyway. Eating organic is the peak of wholesomeness!

The Shop Worker Explains: Ingredients

Saturday afternoon, about one o'clock, and people are stocking up for the weekend at the Red Herring Wholefood Shop. The queue materialises suddenly, spilling out into the corridor to mingle with families coming to the restaurant for a leisurely lunch. At the till the shop worker reaches for loaves of bread, sunlit on their racks from the windows behind. Warm cheesy slices of pizza and golden brown empanadas slip into plastic bags, while fragrant, chewy granary loaves and tender croissants go into paper bags. Someone sets two bottles on the counter: 'What's the difference between tamari and shoyu?' she asks, 'and have you got any tempeh?'

The shop worker sells the bread the bakers bake and talks to the customers. Everything sold in our little shop (from candles to soya yoghurt) or used in the restaurant or bakery is ordered by the shop worker. If you've got questions about ingredients, the shop worker explains. Ever wondered what is the difference between tamari and shoyu, or how they make tempeh? Read on . . .

Meat substitutes

The easiest way to go when you become a vegetarian. Some meat substitutes are very meat-like, while others are less so and help lead one on to adventurous new approaches to cooking.

Texturised Vegetable Protein, or TVP
These popular and easily prepared products come as burger mixes, sausage mixes, soya mince and soya chunks. The're based upon soya bean protein which is the only bean source of all the amino acids required to make complete protein.

Seitan or 'Wheat Meat'
Many find this even meatier than TVP. Most commonly eaten as Chinese Mock Duck, this flavourless product takes its taste from its cooking stock. Pound for pound, seitan is better value than real meat. Only 75g provides over half the Recommended Daily Allowance of useable protein with less than 80 calories, no saturated or hydrogenated fat or cholesterol. Unfortunately if you're gluten sensitive you're out of luck.

Tofu
The soya product most popularly associated with vegetarianism. Reviled as bland, celebrated as versatile, it really depends on how you use it. There are some new, higher quality, tofu products now available using the traditional coagulant, nigari (a mineral extract from sea salt).

There are tasty, firmer-textured varieties such as Clearspot's Age and smoked tofus. Soya milk is curdled with nigari, in a process similar to cheese-making. Use tofu marinaded, baked, fried, barbequed, steamed, or cubed and put into clear soup. Blend it to use as a binder, make scrambled-egg substitute with it, freeze it and squeeze it dry when thawed to make it chewy and meatier in texture. Smooth silken tofu can be whizzed up to make cheesecakes or mixed with melted chocolate and maple syrup to make a vegan icing for cakes.

Tempeh

Savoury, mushroomy tempeh gets strong reactions: either you really like it or you really don't. Tofu was invented in China, tempeh comes from Indonesia. To make it, cooked and hulled soya beans are incubated with koji, a special bacteria that binds the beans together into a cake. The longer the incubation, the stronger the taste. It is sold frozen to arrest incubation and is mildly savoury when predominantly white with darker grey patches. Never eat tempeh with reddish patches on it! You must cook tempeh before eating it, and do so soon after it is thawed. Tempeh is a source of vitamin B_{12}.

Soya products like tofu and tempeh are good natural sources of lecithin, which helps to keep cholesterol from collecting in your arteries.

Special Condiments and Ingredients

Shoyu Soy Sauce is made from fermented soya beans, wheat, salt and water. It's a higher quality product than commercially available soya sauce which is made with chemicals, processed at abnormally high temperatures, artificially aged and artificially coloured.

Tamari Soy Sauce is the liquid that collects on the bottom of the keg during miso making. It contains no wheat, is slightly stronger tasting than shoyu, and doesn't lose any flavour when cooked (shoyu does).

Miso is a savoury paste made from fermenting soya beans, salt, the enzyme starter koji, and sometimes various grains. As it is fermented for years, it can be stored a long time. It is rich in protein and like yoghurt, it's a live food and aids digestion. Buy unpasteurised miso and don't boil it, so the beneficial enzymes aren't destroyed. Dilute and mix with water before adding it to soups, stews and pates.

Nutritional yeast doesn't have the bitter taste associated with brewers' yeast. Its mild cheesy taste contributes to vegan, savoury sauces.

Yeast extract is a concentrated vitamin-rich savoury paste added to soups, nut roasts, sauces, gravies and stews, or spread thinly on bread.

One of the main concerns people have about going vegetarian or vegan is vitamin B_{12}. All the above condiments are sources, as are seaweed, alfalfa sprouts, and dairy products.

Balsamic Vinegar is an Italian vinegar that has been matured in oak sherry casks for up to 20 years. Dark in colour, it has a very special strong, sweet flavour.

Creamed coconut is extracted from pure coconut flesh and compressed into blocks that dissolve easily in hot water. It gives curries and soyps a unique, creamy texture and a subtle coconut flavour.

Kalamata olives are the purple-brown product of Greece, with a rich, pungent flavour. They are distinct from other olives in appearance by the single pointed end. Kalamata olives are cured in brine and are best rinsed before use.

Tahini is a seed butter made from ground sesame seeds and has a smooth texture and strong flavour. As tahini can go rancid and bitter, it's better to get a roasted variety. Roasting prevents rancidness. Also try to get mechanically dehulled tahini, as the hulls contain oxalic acid which makes the tahini's calcium inaccessible to the body. Tahini is either light or dark, depending on the roast. Both are used in sauces and dips and are an excellent binding agent for nut roasts and wholefood biscuits.

Agar agar is a vegetarian gelling agent made from seaweed. Usually available in flakes, it is used for setting jellies, mousses and cheesecakes.

Filo pastry is a paper thin pastry that's popular throughout the middle east. Because it is difficult to make we suggest you buy it ready-made. Filo pastry is used for both sweet and savoury dishes.

Oils

Oil is vital for health. Quality vegetable oil strengthens cells and capillaries, lubricates the skin and hair and actually helps lower blood cholesterol. The best oil is unrefined, cold-pressed and contains nutrients like vitamins A, D and E. It is high in polyunsaturates and thus contributes the essential fatty acids needed for proper metabolism. Oil is needed for the efficient use of B vitamins.

Oil that is mechanically pressed out at low temperatures and simply filtered before bottling retains its vitamins, minerals, flavour and aroma. They are darker and may have sediment. Extra-virgin is the first pressing. Olive, sesame and sunflower oil may all be cold pressed. Harder seeds, grains and beans must be steamed and the oil extracted by screw press. They give less oil but it is still high quality. Highly processed oils are extracted at high temperatures using solvents, and must then be refined to extract the solvent before being bleached and filtered. These oils have a long shelf life but no nutritional content.

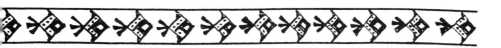

Olive oil is probably the highest quality vegetable oil available, especially if extra-virgin. It keeps for about a year and will go semi-solid if chilled. In this state it can be used to make pastry instead of shortening. It has the least impurities of all oils and aids the absorbtion of vitamins A, D, E and K. Widely regarded to have health-giving properties, it helps digestion. As desirable in cooking as in salads, olive oil doesn't foam or smoke easily when heated.

Sunflower oil is probably the most commonly used oil. It is high in polyunsaturates and not too greasy. It is a good all-purpose oil with a high smoke point and thus good for frying.

Sesame oil is the traditional cooking oil of the far east. It is one of the most unsaturated oils and is ideal for deep frying due to its extremely high smoke point. It is nutritional and mild. Roasted sesame oil is made by pressing roasted sesame seeds and is used as a condiment.

Groundnut (peanut) oil is the best known source of vitamin B_5 (pantothenic acid) and vitamin E. This bland oil is well suited to cooking.

Soya bean oil is nutritious, but strongly flavoured. Better for cooking than for salads, it is not everyone's favourite. Nonetheless, a good source of vitamin E and lecithin.

Sweeteners

Until the Middle Ages, refined sugar was not available in Europe. Initially kept in apothecaries' shops, it eventually became widely used. Sugar is derived from either sugar beets or sugar cane and is not without nutritional merit. Refining sugar removes all the vitamin-and-mineral-rich molasses. The Red Herring uses unrefined sugar. Beware of refined brown sugar that is only white sugar with caramel colouring and a little bit of added molasses! Best of all is to buy unrefined, organic and fair-traded sugar!

Muscovado is a moist, soft brown sugar available in light or dark varieties, depending upon the amount of molasses it retains. It is excellent for baking.

Demerara is a golden granulated sugar that goes well in tea or coffee. It can be used for baking but doesn't dissolve as well as muscovado.

Sugar is addictive, and if you want to cut down there are several options available to you, without resorting to artificial sweeteners.

Grain sweeteners are less sweet than sugar. They metabolise slowly and won't give you a sugar crash and are less addictive. Try barley malt, corn (or maize) malt and brown rice malt. Don't confuse these with refined corn syrup or refined white rice syrup, which is the grain equivalent of white sugar.

Maple syrup is a natural sweetener with a glorious taste. It is very sweet and a little goes a long way. To make one pint of maple syrup takes about forty gallons of maple sap.

Honey is the nectar of flowers which is refined by bees. The nutritional value of pasteurised, refined honey is the same as white sugar, except with more calories. Unpasteurised, unrefined honey is a nutritious thing, made wonderfully so by the bees' contribution of pollen and propolis. Bee pollen is one of the most nutritious foods on the planet and propolis is a naturally healing disinfectant. Honey is sweeter than sugar: use half as much.

Concentrated apple or white grape juice are popular sugar substitutes. They contain many vitamins and minerals from the original fruit. Although they are expensive, they make a wholesome replacement for the liquid sugar, glucose.

Grains

In our meat-centred, fast-food culture, grains are considered boring. Yet grains are the foundation of civilisations, and the development of agriculture was a signpost in human evolution. Across the world, nations thrive on their traditional staple grains.

Rice has nourished the Chinese and Japanese for nearly four thousand years. Likewise in India, rice is eaten. For more than half the world, rice is the staple grain. **Wild rice** is actually from a wild grass harvested by North America's indigenous people, and is not a rice at all.

Wheat, barley, rye and oats are the traditional grains of Britain and northern Europe. Grain was sacred to the Roman goddess Ceres, from whom the word 'cereal' comes.

There are two types of wheat: **hard wheat** which is used to make 'strong' flour and is high in gluten. This is the best flour for bread making and is usually imported from Canada. **Soft wheat** contains more carbohydrate and is used to make pastry flour. English wheat tends to be soft wheat. Bulgar wheat and couscous are both wheat products.

Barley is another ancient grain, eaten for nearly seven thousand years. Egyptians, Chinese, Romans, Hebrews and Greeks all ate barley. Like millet and quinoa, it contains all the amino acids. Barley flour was the main bread making flour before wheat. The hard, heavy loaves were used as edible plates.

Rye is popular in Russia, Scandinavia and Germany. It is usually ground into flour for bread. Low in gluten, it may be tolerated by some people with wheat allergies.

Oats are the staple of Ireland and Scotland. The Roman legions sowed their oats wherever they went across northern Europe. Oats contain more protein and fat than any other grain. Oats are made into oatmeal, porridge oats, oat flour or just whole groats.

Buckwheat is also popular in Russia, but is technically a nut, not a grain. It contains rutin, a substance that strengthens capillary walls, and is a gentle anti-depressant. No doubt this helps people cope with long, dark nights!

Corn or maize is the grain of the Americas. Archaeologists have evidence of it growing wild in Mexico nine thousand years ago. When ground to make tortillas, a pinch of wood ash was added to soften the kernels. this also made more of the amino acids available, without which a corn-centred diet leads to pellagra and kwashiorkor diseases.

Quinoa (pronounced 'keen-wah') was the special grain of the mountain-dwelling Incas. Similar in appearance to millet, it cooks up fluffier and is reputed to be the most nutritious grain of all. Roast it slightly before cooking it.

Millet is popular in Africa, where they also enjoy corn (known there as 'mealie'). Millet has been found in the tombs of the Pharoahs and both Greeks and Romans ate it. It contains all the amino acids and is the staple grain today of northern China. The long-lived Hunza people prefer millet as their grain.

Grain cooking table

The quantities are by volume not weight. Measure the dry grain in cups and add however many times as much water. The yield is in relation to the volume of dry grain.

Grain	Water	Cooking time	Yield
Brown rice	2 x	45 minutes	3 x as much
Polenta (coarse corn meal)	4 x	25 minutes	3 x as much
Quinoa	2 x	15 minutes	2½ x as much
Roasted buckwheat	2 x	15 minutes	2½ x as much
Millet	3 x	45 minutes	3½ x as much
Bulgar wheat	2 x	20 minutes	2½ x as much
Couscous	2 x	15 minutes	2½ x as much
Barley	3 x	75 minutes	3½ x as much
Porridge oats	2 x	15 minutes	2 x as much
Wild rice	3 x	60 minutes	4 x as much

Bulgar wheat and couscous do not have to be cooked. The grain can simply be left to stand in hot or cold water until the water is absorbed. Quinoa should be cooked only until the grain goes transparent; then it too should simply be left to stand until the water is absorbed.

Milk and dairy-like products

The debate over milk is a hot one between vegetarians and vegans. Ethically and nutritionally, vegans have a strong point. Yet we all have a different point where we draw the line in our efforts to live with our conscience. We do our best and learn to live with our decisions.

Milk was the ultimate comfort and safety food when we were children. Most of us in the industrialised western world were brought up drinking milk. It reminds us of childhood and wholesomeness. As cheese it adds subtlety and richness. Regions all have their speciality cheese, developed with distinct tastes to celebrate their uniqueness. Few things are more appealing than a sumptuously steaming mug of hot, creamy chocolate or a bubbling cheese topping, just starting to go crisp and golden. Vegan substitutes simply don't compare. But if you're dedicated, you lose your taste for dairy products. The melted cheese tastes cloying and greasy while the cow's milk tastes of fresh cow pats. You don't notice the beaniness of soya milk any more.

Whatever your choice, make it a positive one. If you drink milk, admit you simply love it and let yourself take pleasure in it. If you're vegan, persist and feel proud of your decision.

Dairy substitutes

If you've decided not to include milk in your diet there are a lot of options. Take heart: you'll lose your taste for dairy products over time. It may take a while to phase it out, but if you're persistent and not too hard on yourself it will happen.

Soya milk is soon to be re-named 'soya drink' due to an E.C. ruling. However you can do more than drink it. You can cook with it, if you keep the heat and acidity low to prevent curdling. You can make hot chocolate with soya milk and its beany taste is well masked in coffee – just remember to pour your soya milk in before the coffee. Soya milk is made from dehulled soya beans ground up with water and strained.

Rice milk is an alternative for those who don't like soya milk. It doesn't really go in tea or coffee and is not much use in cooking. However, it is naturally sweet and tastes great on muesli.

Oat milk is a new development that is most suited to cooking.

Soya cream is a non-dairy alternative to pouring cream. The taste and texture can be fairly convincing, depending on the brand, but it has a high fat content like the real thing.

Soya yoghurt varies a lot from brand to brand. Few of them are actually cultured like yoghurt, but you can find live soya yoghurt. They you can use it as a starter to make your own with soya milk.

Soya cheese is not always vegan. It tends to be disappointing, though there is a convincing vegan cream cheese on the market.

Eggs and egg replacers

A miracle food in its own package, eggs are second only to human breast milk in protein availability. 98% of the protein in eggs is in a useable form, compared to 60% of meat protein. There are, however, some concerns. Few vegetarians are comfortable with the idea of battery hens. Besides the ethics, there is the problem of the antibiotics and yellow pigment these hens are fed passing into the eggs in concentrated form. free range eggs don't have this problem, though it's important to be sure they're the real thing, not battery eggs labelled 'farm fresh'!

Eggs also have a high cholesterol content. One egg contains 275mg of cholesterol; the recommended daily limit is 300mg. On the other hand, eggs also contain lecithin, which prevents cholesterol from being deposited in the arteries. As long as you don't cook them swimming in oil, eggs probably aren't too bad for you.

Egg replacers

Whether you're a vegan or allergic to eggs, you may choose not to eat them. There are alternatives. You just need to identify what the egg in a recipe is for and find something else to do the job.

Plain tofu can be used for your morning scrambled eggs.

Commercial egg replacers can be used in baking, though they can be expensive.

Rising agent can be increased in baking, and a little more oil or soya milk added.

Agar agar or **silken tofu** can be used to set a cheesecake or a mousse.

Soya flour binds batters together.

Tahini sticks nut roasts and burgers together nicely.

Flour or cornflour made into a thin paste and cooked also binds burgers and roasts.

If you make a vegan cake be aware that it will be heavier and less springy than its eggy counterpart. Grease and line your pans with circles of grease-proof paper, and remove it when the cake is cold. Let the cakes cool completely in their pans. If your vegan cake won't come out of its tin, freeze it in the tin. Then warm the bottom of the tin on a stove for a few seconds, slide a knife round the edge and turn out the cake, tapping its bottom.

Tips and Techniques

We've included both quick and easy dishes and more complex ones in *Cordon Rouge*. Some may take more thought and time to prepare but none are really very difficult. In any case, all dishes are more likely to be a success if you do two things:

READ THE WHOLE RECIPE FIRST!

This will make sure you've got all the ingredients, understand the techniques and can do any necessary advance preparations. Guesswork can lead to culinary disasters.

DO THE ADVANCE PREPARATION!

Dried beans need to be soaked, tempeh may need to be marinaded . . . Also, many accompaniments can be prepared in advance (vinaigrette is an obvious example). Dips and pates are often better after they have had a day to let the flavours 'bloom', and because they become firmer. Pastry benefits from time in the fridge, becoming easier to roll and more tender when baked.

Advance preparation includes washing, peeling and chopping vegetables. There's no point in burning your onions while you're trying to quickly chop the carrots and broccoli before adding them!

Washing and preparing vegetables

Much of the mineral and vitamin content of vegetables is concentrated next to the skins. Unfortunately, so are the chemical residues of pesticides and fertilisers. Unless you buy or grow organic produce, peel your vegetables instead of just washing them.

If you use organic vegetables, you'll find yourself using local, seasonal vegetables a lot more. Remember that you don't have to adhere strictly to what a recipe tells you to use, and you can substitute one vegetable for another.

If you use the **fresh herbs** many of our recipes recommend, you'll find it easier to put them in a cup and snip them up with scissors rather than using a knife and chopping board.

Fresh garlic is easier to peel if you crush the cloves slightly with the flat of a knife.

Aubergines require special preparation to soften them and extract their bitter juices. After slicing the aubergine, place it in a colander and sprinkle the pieces with salt. Let it stand for about half an hour and then rinse it thoroughly. It can then be cooked like any other vegetable.

Soaking beans and pulses

All beans except aduki beans and mung beans need to be soaked overnight in three times their volume of water. Lentils and split peas do not need soaking either. Drain off the soak water and replace with fresh water before cooking. Do not add salt until after the beans are cooked as it toughens them. A piece of kombu seaweed cooked with the beans helps to soften them.

Cooking times for beans

These are approximate times only

Lentils and split peas	30–45 minutes
Aduki beans and mung beans	45 minutes
Black-eyed beans	1½ hours
Butterbeans (Lima beans)	1½ hours
Cannelini beans	1½ hours
Chickpeas	3 hours
Flageolet beans	1 hour
Haricot beans	2½ hours
Kidney beans	1½ hours
Pinto beans	2½ hours

A pressure cooker reduces cooking times for beans considerably and eliminates the need to soak. Consult the instructions with your pressure cooker (if you have got one) for pressure cooking times.

Equipment

A restaurant obviously has access to equipment you may not have, like a food processor. We use one to blend soups and sauces, chop nuts, make breadcrumbs and whizz up pates. It is useful but expensive and not essential. Hummus can be mashed, tapenade made in a mortar and pestle or put through a sieve with the back of a spoon. Nuts can be put into a plastic bag and bashed with a rolling pin (gently!). If you dry out your bread you can make breadcrumbs this way too. If you chop your vegetables finely and simmer until they're tender, you don't really need to blend soups. Whether you blend soup or not is a matter of personal taste.

A sieve, a chopping board (not a glass 'counter-saver' which blunts knives), kitchen scissors and a mortar and pestle are nice to have. The scissors are great for herbs but not essential. The mortar and pestle are wonderful for grinding whole spices like roasted cumin seeds, but also not essential.

Your most important utensil has got to be a sharp knife. A large one for chopping lots of hard vegetables and a small one for seeding peppers and peeling fruit is ideal. Keep your knives sharp! You are more likely to cut yourself with a dull knife than a sharp one. Remember not to leave them lurking in the bottom of a soapy sink and carry them point downwards.

Cooking methods

Cooking affects the appearance, taste and texture of food. While it develops the flavour, it also destroys many nutrients in the process. Most nutrients are not heat stable. Some cooking philosophies, like macrobiotics, feel that the process of cooking imparts new energies to the food to balance this. Perhaps the best approach is to cook your food with care, and to eat fresh, uncooked food like fruit and salad, too.

Steaming and boiling vegetables can leach out water soluble nutrients. Try just covering your vegetables in water when you boil them, and keep the water for soup stock. Steaming takes out fewer nutrients than boiling; remember to keep the lid on to prevent those vitamins from evaporating into the air.

Pasta requires more water than vegetables so it doesn't stick to itself. Eleanor's rules for perfect pasta are to add the pasta to water that has reached boiling point, and to add a little oil to prevent it from sticking together.

Grains need exact quantities of water. Ideally, all the water should be absorbed into the grain, which remains light and tender.

Frying and sauteing mean cooking food quickly and lightly in a little oil, so as not to lose oil soluble nutrients. The oil should be hot but not smoking (apparently this is carcinogenic) when you add the food so it doesn't stick to the pan. Brown the food then lower the temperature so it can cook through, stirring occasionally. Often onions and garlic are fried to begin a recipe. Add the onions first to hot oil (so they don't stick or go soggy) and when they go translucent add the garlic. Garlic needs only a few minutes to cook and burns easily.

Stir-frying uses less oil and the natural moisture already in the vegetables. Keep the heat on medium-low and stir constantly, coating the food with the oil. A little salt helps to extract the vegetables' moisture. Add the vegetables in order of hardness (carrots first, mushrooms last, etc.). Tenderise at the end with a few tablespoons of water and put a lid on to keep in the steam.

Deep-frying is messy and increases the fat content of food. Nevertheless, for some things (like stilton croquettes) it is the best way to achieve the right effect. The oil must be hot enough to brown (without burning) or the food will absorb it and be soggy, not crisp. Try a test piece first. Don't let the oil smoke, or overfill the pan. The more food you put into the oil at once, the more quickly its temperature will drop.

Braising combines moist and dry heat. First, food is browned to seal in flavour, then a liquid (such as stock) is added and the food is slowly simmered until tender. Indonesian vegetable curry is braised for maximum flavour.

Broiling and grilling quick-cook food with an exposed heat source like a flame or oven element that browns the food's surface. When broiling or grilling vegetarian-style, remember to lightly coat the food in oil to keep it moist.

Roasting is a slow cooking method that uses dry heat, usually in an oven. It tenderises food and allows flavours to develop over time. Vegetarian roasting is best done in a covered dish to prevent drying out. Nut roasts generally need to be covered for the majority of their cooking time and browned for ten minutes at the end.

Toasting enhances the flavour of nuts and seeds. Each variety should be toasted in a separate pan as the toasting time varies. Red skin peanuts, brazil nuts and hazelnuts all need about 10 minutes in a moderate oven. Flaked almonds, seeds, cashews and pine kernels need only about 5 minutes. You'll need to experiment with your own oven and preferences.

Add a tablespoon of shoyu to your seeds (like pumpkin or sunflower) and stir them occasionally until the shoyu has completely dried onto the seeds. This is a fabulous snack.

'Gomasio' is a savoury condiment made from sesame seeds. Roast 125g sesame seeds with ½ tsp salt until the seeds are golden. They continue cooking for a few minutes after you've taken them from the oven and darken a little more. Grind them in a mortar and pestle (or blender) until the hulls are cracked and powdery. Sprinkle it over rice, vegetables, or anything savoury.

Weights and Measures

In this book the measurements are given in their metric form. The following tables provide conversions for those using imperial values.

Weight Conversion Table			Volume Conversion Table	
Imperial	**Metric**		**Imperial**	**Metric**
Ounces	Grammes		Fluid ounces	Millilitres
1	25		1	25
2	50		2	50
3	75		3	75
4 (¼ lb)	100		4	125
5	150		5 (¼ pint)	150
6	175		6	175
7	200		7	200
8 (½ lb)	225		8	225
9	250		9	250
10	275		10 (½ pint)	300
11	325		11	325
12 (¾ lb)	350		12	350
13	375		13	375
14	400		15 (¾ pint)	450
15	425		20 (1 pint)	600
16 (1 lb)	450			

Oven Temperatures

	°C	°F	Gas Mark
	70	150	
	80	175	
	100	200	
Very cool	110	225	¼
	120	250	½
	140	275	1
Cool	150	300	2
Warm	170	325	3
Moderate	180	350	4
	190	375	5
	200	400	6
Hot	220	425	7
	230	450	8
Very hot	250	500	9

Abbreviations

g	gramme
kg	kilogram
lb	pound
oz	ounce
fl oz	fluid ounce
l	litre
ml	millilitre
tsp	teaspoon
tbsp	tablespoon
cm	centimetre
mm	millimetre

The Red Herring's Roots

The original Red Herring Cafe opened in a downstairs Tyneside flat on Dilston Road sometime in 1981 as a bit of an anarchic experiment. I borrowed £5 from eight people and bought some second hand crockery and cutlery, a water boiler, some pans and chairs. The trestle tables were made from internal doors removed and replaced with a curtain. There was no indication from the outside that it was a cafe and no obligation to pay, only a bowl for contributions 'to world revolution'. We told people it was a cafe and they started to visit. It was interesting and chaotic, the kitchen was tiny and the food fairly basic.

No one got paid, we just wanted to see what came of it. There was some anti-fascist activity in the area and contributions were made to the first 'reclaim the night' marches. I lived on the premises and kept things going with support from various dedicated people.

Sometimes I would be persuaded to go down the pub to get away from it. We left the lights on, the door unlocked and a note explaining what food was on and where everything was. When we came back people had been in and helped themselves to food and there was more money in the bowl than when we left! That sort of thing made it all worthwhile.

Someone said, 'Well, it's a bit of a Red Herring because it doesn't really look like a cafe'. That's what it became and we've used the name ever since. I had a degree in agricultural economics but had never grown a vegetable myself. I realised that I had to feed myself before I could help anyone else very much. For me it was a bit of a Red Herring because really it was a means of learning and sharing skills so I might ultimately help others.

The first Red Herring left me with a major discovery and realisation: I had found a way, more or less, whatever else happened, that I could house and feed myself. I could always find somewhere to offer food and warmth for people and it would provide enough to feed me and keep a roof over my head. If the cafe were closed down for any reason it could easily open somewhere else with little capital or risk. We had ideas for 'guerilla cafes' perhaps opened in a shut down shop – get in there overnight, open for breakfast the following morning and sustain it for as long as one could, a day or a month or perhaps longer. We've still never done that but I hope people will some day – let me know if you do it, I'd like to come along.

In those youthful days of idealism we thought it might be possible to change the world. I came to believe something which has driven me

on ever since: that to convert an idea to reality is a liberation and an inspiration. To do something concrete as an expression of an idea is more powerful than simply reiterating the idea ad nauseam, however insignificant the concrete reality. I wanted to change the world but the most I could do was to start a cafe, opening my door to the world to see if it would enter and perhaps discuss further initiatives that might just make a difference.

When I wanted to move on, take a trip to Barcelona, to meet some anarchists actually, I hoped the cafe might keep going but it didn't quite happen. I was O.K. about that and felt I didn't have to be too attached to it. With £40 in my pocket I got as far as Paris. After only a fortnight I hitched home with my tail between my legs.

I came back to Newcastle and made an Easter cycling trip to the Lakes. On the way back I sorted out a summer job at the Village Bakery in Melmerby. Initially I was just gardening and stoking the wood fired oven, but soon I was in the bakery more or less full time. It gave me my enthusiasm for the brick oven and baking. I was tempted to stay but in October 1982 I decided that I needed to get involved in something of my own or together with like-minded folk. Back in Newcastle, I meditated and made bread. People knocked on the door and bought it. I thought, 'If I had a larger oven could I earn my living from baking?'

At this time I was involved in non-violent direct action against the military and arms industry and felt moved to be involved in ever more dramatic ways. Realising that at this rate I could soon be imprisoned for some not-so-non-violent anti-war activity, I decided to get off the dole and try to bring my way of life and my beliefs together to make bread not bombs. If I ever earned enough to pay tax I would join the Peace Tax Campaign and withhold the income tax until I got an assurance it would not be used for military purposes.

I set about planning and eventually building an oven in my backyard. I didn't really know what I was doing. It had to be simple. Eventually I built one with great help from Pete Burn, a jack of all trades. I started baking in October 1985. Fortuitously, some folk had started a wholefood shop around the corner. They called it 'Eddie's Wholefood Emporium' after the cat. When they discovered I was building an oven they asked me if I would supply them with bread and soon other shops wanted it too. After a year or so the people at Eddie's asked if I would go in with them to open a cafe in the unused space at the back, sharing the overheads half and half. I agreed and started work on the premises in November 1986, eventually fixing a date for opening on February 28th 1987! The Red Herring of today was spawned.   *Nigel Wild*

Soups

Perhaps the most popular dish at the Red Herring is the soup of the day. This section contains some of the favourites, including courgette and cumin, lentil and coconut and curried parsnip.

The ingredients used in each recipe give the soup its distinctive flavour, texture and colour. Although each soup is very different they are all full of flavour and highly nutritious.

The Red Herring always tries to ensure that vegans are provided with as many dishes as vegetarians. Because of this the soups on the menu are always vegan. There is also the option of incorporating individual preferences into all of the recipes. Obviously people's tastes do vary and the addition of yoghurt, milk or cheese can create soups with very different tastes and textures.

When serving any of the soups there are also the accompaniments to be considered. Favourites at the Red Herring are garlic bread, hot cheddar or stilton stuffed croissants and freshly baked rolls.

Customers enjoying the atmosphere and a beverage in the cafe.

Broccoli and Almond
Comfort soup.

Celery and Cashew
Peppery celery with the rich nuttiness of cashews. Make it even better with a handful of chopped spicy, lemony lovage leaves.

Armenian (Red Lentil and Apricot)
An unusual combination of sweet and savoury but the other ingredients ensure that it is not too sweet – especially the parsley, which gives it that extra something.

Celso (Mediterranean Bean)
A specific, warm Mediterranean taste. Make it in the winter and reminisce about your last summer holiday. . .

Minestrone
From Italy, the classic hearty soup.

Lentil and Coconut
One of our most popular, it's surprisingly easy and deliciously filling.

Pumpkin and Ginger
Lively and sweet, with a gentle bite.

Red Pepper and Tomato
Rich, vibrant colour and well-rounded flavour.

Chestnut Potage
Festive and seasonally special.

Carrot and Orange
Bright and zingy to wake up your tastebuds.

Borscht
Sweet, rosy-red beetroot in a distinctive eastern European soup.

Curried Parsnip
Winter soup to warm and satisfy.

Courgette and Cumin
The delicate taste of courgettes enhanced by the haunting bite of fresh roasted cumin seeds.

Broccoli and Almond Soup

serves 4-6
vegan
contains nuts

1 tbsp	sunflower oil
2	small onions (chopped)
2	sticks of celery (chopped)
150g	flaked almonds
1 l	vegetable stock
1	head of broccoli (chopped)
1 tsp	mustard powder
	salt and pepper
	ground nutmeg to garnish

Fry the onion, celery and almonds in the oil until the almonds brown.

Add the stock and the broccoli and bring to the boil.

Add the mustard powder and cook until the broccoli is tender.

Alllow to cool slightly and blend until smooth.

Reheat and check seasoning.

Celery and Cashew Soup

serves 4-6
vegan
contains nuts

50g	margarine
2	medium onions (chopped)
2	medium potatoes (chopped)
1	head of celery (chopped)
125g	broken cashews (toasted)
1 l	vegetable stock
	salt and pepper

Melt the margarine and fry the onion, potato and celery.

Add the cashew nuts and cook for 5 minutes.

Add the vegetable stock, bring to the boil, then cover and simmer for 20 minutes.

Allow to cool slightly and blend.

Reheat and check seasoning.

Armenian Soup

serves 4-6

Red lentil and apricot

vegan

'I've got a theory that this soup has special magical healing properties for body, mind and soul (and hangovers!). In any case, I think I can safely say that it's very good for you – lots of iron and B vitamins. When I used to write this one on the blackboard at the Red Herring, people would murmur 'red lentil and apricot? red lentil and apricot?' to each other.'

Hannah Rye

50g	*red lentils (washed)*
50g	*dried apricots (chopped)*
1	*large potato (chopped)*
1 l	*vegetable stock*
	juice of ½ a lemon
1 tsp	*ground cumin*
2 tbsp	*chopped fresh parsley*
	salt and pepper

Place lentils, apricots and potato in a pan with the stock, lemon juice and cumin.

Bring to the boil, cover and simmer for 30 minutes until the potato·is tender and the lentils are cooked.

Allow to cool slightly and then blend the soup until smooth.

Add the chopped parsley, reheat and check seasoning before serving.

Celso or Mediterranean Bean Soup

serves 4-6

vegan

350g	*haricot or cannellini beans (soaked overnight)*
1 l	*vegetable stock made with tomato stock cubes*
2	*small onions (finely chopped)*
3	*sticks celery (finely chopped)*
2 tsp	*chopped fresh basil*
2 tsp	*chopped fresh parsley*
400g	*tin chopped tomatoes*
3 tbsp	*olive oil*
	salt and pepper

Drain the soaked beans, rinse well, then place in a pan of fresh water and cook until tender. Drain, reserving the cooking water.

Place the cooked beans in a pan with the tomato stock. If the tomato stock does not cover the beans, add some of the bean stock to ensure the liquid covers the beans.

Add the onions, celery, basil, parsley, tomatoes and olive oil and bring to the boil, then cover.

Simmer over a low heat for 20-30 minutes until the vegetables are soft. Season to taste.

Minestrone Soup

serves 4-6

vegan

1 tbsp	oil
1	onion (finely chopped)
2	sticks of celery (finely chopped)
1	clove of garlic (crushed)
1	small tin of chopped tomatoes
1	bay leaf
½ tsp	dried oregano
1 tsp	fresh or dried basil
¼ tsp	dried rosemary
1	green pepper (finely chopped)
2	carrots (finely chopped)
2	courgettes (finely chopped)
1 l	vegetable stock
2 tbsp	tomato puree
25g	noodles, spaghetti or vermicelli
1 tsp	salt
2 tsp	soy sauce
1 tbsp	chopped fresh parsley
	salt and pepper

Fry the onion, garlic and celery until soft.

Add the tomatoes, herbs, vegetables, stock and tomato puree. Bring to the boil; then simmer for 40 minutes.

Add noodles, soy sauce and salt and pepper and simmer until the noodles or pasta are soft.

Garnish with fresh parsley before serving.

Lentil and Coconut Soup

serves 4-6
vegan

2 tbsp	oil
2	onions (finely chopped)
300g	washed red lentils
1 l	water
1	block of creamed coconut
1	chilli (de-seeded and finely chopped)
1	small red pepper (finely chopped)
1 tbsp	cumin seeds (roasted, then finely ground)
3 tsp	chopped fresh coriander or fresh parsley
	juice of one lemon
	salt and pepper

Fry the onion until soft.

Add the washed lentils and water and cook for 10-15 minutes until the lentils are tender.

Add the coconut, chilli, cumin and red pepper; then cook for 5 minutes.

Stir in the chopped herbs and lemon juice.

Season to taste.

Pumpkin and Ginger Soup

serves 4-6
vegan

2 kg	pumpkin
50g	margarine
2	onions (finely chopped)
4 tsp	grated fresh ginger
600 ml	soya milk
2 tbsp	sugar
1½ tsp	nutmeg
	fresh chives to garnish

Remove the skin and seeds, then cut the pumpkin into cubes.

Heat the margarine and fry the onion and ginger until soft. Then add the pumpkin and cook for 5 minutes, stirring frequently.

Pour in the milk, bring to the boil, then add the sugar and nutmeg. Simmer until the pumpkin is tender.

Allow to cool slightly, then blend. Check the seasoning.

To serve, reheat and garnish with chopped chives and, for non-vegans, a swirl of sour cream.

Red Pepper and Tomato Soup

serves 4-6

vegan

2 tbsp	oil
1	onion (finely chopped)
1	red pepper (finely chopped)
1	carrot (finely chopped)
1	stick celery (finely chopped)
1	potato (finely chopped)
½ tsp	paprika
½ tsp	ground ginger
½ tsp	thyme
350 ml	vegetable stock
4 tbsp	tomato puree
1 tsp	sugar
1 tsp	salt
1 tsp	cornflour
1 tsp	plain flour
4 tbsp	soya milk
3-4	fresh tomatoes (finely chopped)
1 tbsp	chopped fresh parsley

Heat the oil and saute the vegetables for 10 minutes. Then add the spices and mix well.

Add the stock, tomato puree, sugar and salt and bring to the boil. Simmer for 15 minutes until the vegetables are tender.

Mix the cornflour and plain flour with the soya milk and add it to the hot soup. Stir until the soup thickens.

Remove from the heat and add tomatoes and parsley. Check seasoning and blend if required.

Chestnut Potage

serves 4-6
vegan
contains nuts

350g	dried chestnuts (soaked overnight)
4 tbsp	oil
4	sticks celery (finely chopped)
½	small green cabbage (finely chopped)
2	onions (finely chopped)
1 l	vegetable stock
1	bay leaf
½ tsp	thyme
1 tsp	marjoram
150 ml	dry cider
	salt and pepper

Drain and rinse the chestnuts, then boil in fresh water and simmer for 20-30 minutes until they are tender.

Heat the oil and fry the celery, cabbage and onion until golden.

Add the cooked chestnuts and the vegetable stock and bring to the boil. Add the herbs and seasoning; then cover and simmer for 15-20 minutes.

Add the cider, allow to cool slightly, then blend until smooth.

Reheat and serve.

Carrot and Orange Soup

serves 4-6
vegan

2 tbsp	oil
1	onion (chopped)
1 kg	carrots (chopped)
1 l	vegetable stock
½ tsp	nutmeg
½ tsp	paprika
5 tbsp	chopped fresh coriander
	zest and juice of 1 large orange
	salt and pepper

Heat the oil and add the chopped onion and saute for 2-3 minutes on a low heat until the onion is soft.

Add the carrots and saute for a further 10 minutes.

Add the stock, spices and coriander with the orange zest and juice. Bring to the boil and simmer for 40 minutes.

Allow to cool slightly and blend until smooth.

Reheat and check seasoning.

Borscht

serves 4-6

vegan

'This is one of my favourites but it does seem that people love it or hate it. I love the shocking deep rich colour and the thick texture as well as the flavour. I find it hard to resist a swirl of yoghurt in it which is such a brilliant contrast!'   *Nigel*

2 tbsp	oil
1	medium onion (chopped)
500g	raw beetroot (peeled and chopped)
1	medium potato (chopped)
1	medium carrot (chopped)
1	medium cooking apple (chopped)
850 ml	vegetable stock
½ tsp	cumin
½ tsp	nutmeg
2 tbsp	red wine
	salt and pepper

Heat the oil and fry the onion until soft.

Add the potato, beetroot, carrot and apple and cook for 5–10 minutes.

Add the stock and bring to the boil. Add the cumin and nutmeg and simmer until the vegetables are tender.

Season and add the red wine.

Allow to cool and blend until smooth.

Reheat and check seasoning.

Curried Parsnip Soup

serves 6-8

vegan

50g	*margarine*
1	*onion (chopped)*
1 kg	*parsnips (chopped)*
500g	*potatoes (chopped)*
2 tsp	*curry powder*
½ tsp	*ground cumin*
1 l	*vegetable stock*
	salt and pepper

Fry the chopped onion, potatoes and parsnip in the margarine for 2-3 minutes until the onion is soft.

Add the cumin and curry powder and cook for 2 minutes, stirring well to avoid the spices burning.

Add the stock and bring to the boil, then cover and simmer for 30-40 minutes until the vegetables are tender.

Cool slightly and blend. Reheat and check seasoning.

Courgette and Cumin Soup

serves 4-6

vegan

50g	*margarine*
1	*large onion (chopped)*
3	*cloves of garlic (chopped)*
750g	*potatoes (chopped)*
1kg	*courgettes (chopped)*
3 tsp	*ground cumin*
1 tsp	*paprika*
1 l	*vegetable stock*

Saute the onion and garlic in the margarine.

Stir in the spices.

Add the chopped potatoes and courgettes.

Add the vegetable stock and cook until the vegetables are soft.

Allow to cool slightly and blend.

Reheat and check seasoning.

Early Days

I worked incredibly long hours – often seven days a week – but I did have support and help from some very good people. Among them, Andy Knight and Aidan shared the anxiety and difficulties, working way beyond what anyone could reasonably expect for occasional payments. We always struggled to keep the fire going in the oven, to get it hot enough, to rebuild the grate after the last collapse, to keep the old van going. There were always repairs and improvements, always shopping to do because we couldn't afford to buy anything except flour in bulk. Their help allowed me to plan and work on the cafe whilst we still made the bread, pasties, pizza, quiche and croissants which were our staples. These were delivered around town in an old splitscreen VW van which had a penchant for breaking down on Newcastle's busiest roundabout.

We planned the cafe with the three partners of Eddie's Wholefood Emporium. They were to put £1,000 in and me and Andy between us would also put in £1,000 to see how far that would get us. None of us had any money, except we had just done a week's catering job for 'The Standing Conference on Young People's Theatre'. Remarkably, we'd earned enough to stand our £1,000. Unfortunately, the others changed their minds, so it was our only capital. We decided to press on regardless, trusting that somehow we would find a way.

The premises were unusual. There had always been a shopfront; for many years it was a grocery shop and a woman lived in the back, bringing up her children in there. Apart from the shop there was a kitchen with a range, two bedrooms, an outside privy and a coalhouse. Interestingly, she had baked bread on the range for sale in the shop, some eighty years ago. Her demise came through not being able to get a beer licence; she was allowed a spirits licence but at the time beer was more difficult to obtain a licence for and they were licenced separately.

The old kitchen was to become a cafe. One of the bedrooms was to become a kitchen with a serving hatch knocked through between them. Water, gas and drainage needed providing. Writing it makes it seem so straightforward but all these things caused major problems. Once again, Pete Burn was recruited to help, along with Timmo Thompson. They did so on a very reasonable basis and, generously, were prepared to be paid when we could afford it. We made the initial £1,000 do a lot. Other money was raised from friends and supporters. I printed a loan share certificate on an old printing press I had acquired. It promised to repay the bearer in food or cash with interest of food, beverages etc. Altogether nearly another £1,000 was raised this way.

I'd had a friendly architect adapt the planning drawings which were initially submitted by Eddie's. The City Council's planning department very helpfully agreed it should be accepted as an extension of the activities agreed in the original plans. As such we would not need to apply for permission. It was a major coup. We had all been anxious about this. To satisfy the building inspectors, we did things and re-did things. We had to knock out fireplaces and the remnants of the old range with a hundred years of soot, old lime mortar and rubble. The old range and chimney breast itself was a whole skipful carefully removed so as not to collapse the whole chimney. It was then partially rebuilt to provide for a coke stove Pete had made to heat the space.

At some point after New Year 1987 I decided we needed a deadline to focus our minds. I set on Saturday, February 28th to have a grand opening so we could be shut on Sunday and Monday to sort things out for our first full week starting Tuesday 3rd March, Shrove Tuesday!

We had some good fortune and a friend who worked at the Gulbenkian Theatre rang one day to let us know the whole of the stage was being replaced. There was masses of wood to be had free, thanks to the RSC. We got two van loads and made three splendid trestle tables, in a development of the doors as tables of the first Red Herring. The arrangement maximised seating but also generated a degree of communality. People had to sit close together, squeezed up with other couples or parties.

The tables were finished only on the eve of the opening. We didn't have a cooker either until three days before. We could not afford a catering cooker but I had in mind a large domestic cooker called a Carron Cordon Bleu. Literally three days before opening I found one advertised in the paper and drove out one wet and windy evening to try and strike a deal. They are very expensive, at the time around £1,000 new. The bloke who opened the door took us to an outhouse where it was stored. It was in quite good condition. He told us if we preferred they had the same model but all electric. They'd originally had that one and liked it but thought they'd prefer a gas version. So they'd bought a gas version, which they were delighted with, except for one or two features which they preferred on the electric one. They'd then acquired a third one – half electric and half gas. They were left with the all gas and all electric ones to sell. I stated my preference for gas and asked how much he wanted for it. 'Oh dear, I'm dreadful at this sort of thing, how about £60?' Such a bargain, I could hardly believe it, but being skint I said, 'I don't mean to offend and I think it's a very fair price but would you consider £50? We'd be very happy to entertain your family to a full meal when we are open'. He accepted and helped us on our way a good deal.   *Nigel Wild*

Starters

The Red Herring's menu always offers a variety of different starters for both vegetarians and vegans. All the starters are unique in their flavours and ingredients, which makes them ideal for a wide range of menus, tastes and seasons.

Because it is the starter that opens a meal, they have the important task of stimulating taste buds so that appetites are increased for the following courses. Their other main purpose is to offer the eater a taste of what is to come, a mouthwatering starter means that the main course will be awaited with eager anticipation.

Selecting a starter to accompany a main dish does require some thought as certain starters and main dishes complement each other better than others. One basic rule to follow is not to choose a starter with similar ingredients to the main course. For example, stilton stuffed mushrooms would not be a starter to go with nutty mushroom and stilton crumble. A variety of flavours makes a meal far more interesting. It is also a good idea to put a light starter with a sumptuous main course so that the diner's appetite is not lost halfway through the meal.

All of the starters chosen for this section can easily be adapted to form meals in themselves. Portion sizes can be increased and serving breads and salads alongside the starter can create anything from a light snack to a satisfying supper dish. Many also make wonderful sandwich fillings. Most starters can be made, refrigerated and used over a period of days.

From
Borrowed   pounds
in good faith
for six months or so,
to build a cafe,
The Red Herring,
at 4, Studley Terrace.
Will pay back,
preferably, with food
to the value of   pounds
or in cash with
simple interest of
a fine beverage!
With thanks.

Nigel
feb '87

A copy of an original share certificate which raised £1,000. Nigel did the lino cut fish, typeset the text and printed it on an old treadle platen.

Spicy Garlic and Almond Dip
An easy to make starter, delicious served with crunchy crudites.

Stilton and Walnut Dip
Rich and creamy with a refreshing lift from fresh pears.

Hummus
This popular vegan chickpea dip is creamy and flavoured with lemon and garlic.

Tapenade
The recipe you've all been waiting for. A black kalamata olive and ground almond pate which can convert non-olive lovers forever.

Guacamole
A deliciously spicy avocado dip; the fresh coriander and chillis give it the flavours of South America.

Roasted Red Pepper and Almond Dip
A colourful, flavourful starter to stimulate the tastebuds.

Flatcap Mushroom Pate
A creamy mushroom pate.

Stilton Stuffed Mushrooms
A starter for special occasions. Flatcap mushrooms with a delicious stilton filling, grilled until golden and bubbling.

Falafel
Middle Eastern style chickpea fritters.

Parsnip and Sweetcorn Fritters
The sweet flavour of these fritters is complemented by serving with a yogurt dressing.

Mixed Nut Balls
Special, savoury morsels best served with a piquant dip.

Vegetable Kebabs
Vegetables combined for a wide range of tastes, colours and textures. An ideal starter for summer barbeques.

Patlican Tava
A Middle Eastern starter of oven roasted aubergines topped with a sweet and sour fresh tomato and currant sauce and a generous sprinkling of pine kernels.

Mixed Vegetable Pakoras
A traditional Indian dish. The crispy spicy coating contrasts with the succulent vegetables. Delicious dipped in a spicy sauce.

Spicy Garlic and Almond Dip

serves 4-6
vegan
contains nuts

1½g	*ground almonds*
1	*clove garlic (crushed)*
¼ tsp	*chilli powder*
1	*pinch salt*
2	*tomatoes (skinned and roughly chopped)*
2 tbsp	*red wine vinegar*
150 ml	*olive oil*

Put the almonds, garlic, chilli powder, salt, tomatoes and vinegar into a liquidiser and blend until smooth.

Whilst liquidiser is operating, add oil slowly through the hole in the lid. The mixture will gradually thicken.

Chill for at least 2 hours before serving to allow the mixture to thicken and flavours to develop.

Serve as a dip with crudites (vegetable sticks) and herb and onion bread, or use with mayonnaise as a salad dressing.

Stilton and Walnut Pate with Pears

serves 4-6
contains nuts

250g	*stilton cheese (grated)*
375g	*cottage cheese*
100 ml	*milk*
5	*pears (peeled, cored and finely sliced)*
	juice of 1 lemon
40g	*walnuts (chopped)*

Mix the stilton, cottage cheese and milk to form a smooth, creamy consistency.

Place the sliced pears in a bowl and gently toss in the lemon juice.

To serve, place the cheese mixture in a large ramekin and top with the slices of pear and chopped walnuts. Eat with bread or melba toast.

Hummus

serves 4-6
vegan

250g	*chickpeas (soaked overnight)*
4 tbsp	*light tahini*
	juice of 1 lemon
4	*cloves garlic (crushed)*
	salt

Drain the soaked chickpeas, rinse well and boil in fresh water until soft. When cooked, drain the chickpeas, reserving the cooking stock.

Chop the garlic in a blender, then add the chickpeas, lemon, tahini and enough of the cooking liquid to give a smooth consistency.

Add the olive oil and blend well. Then season with salt, and allow to cool before serving.

Serve in a ramekin with garlic bread, or to make a more substantial dish, add crudites, selected from cucumber, carrot, celery, baby turnip, peppers and spring onions. Garnish the hummus with an olive and paprika mixed with olive oil.

Tapenade

serves 8
vegan
contains nuts

500g	*kalamata olives (stoned)*
1-2	*chillis (finely chopped)*
3	*cloves garlic (crushed)*
1/2 tsp	*grated nutmeg*
3 tbsp	*shoyu*
4 tbsp	*wine vinegar*
1 tbsp	*yeast extract*
120 ml	*olive oil*
2	*large pinches of dried tarragon*
2 tsp	*sugar*
250g	*ground almonds*
	salt and pepper

Chop the garlic and chillis in a blender and then add the stoned olives and blend again.

Add the spices, shoyu, vinegar, yeast extract, oil and sugar and blend well.

Finally, add the ground almonds and pepper and blend to a smooth texture. If the mix is too wet add more ground almonds until the desired texture is reached.

Serve with herb and onion bread.

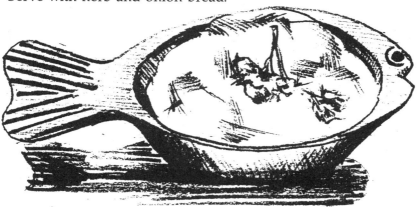

Guacamole

serves 4-6

vegan

2	large ripe avocadoes
3 tbsp	chopped fresh coriander
4	firm tomatoes (finely chopped)
1-2	fresh chillis (finely chopped)
1	small onion (very finely chopped)
	salt and pepper
	lemon to garnish

Prepare the tomatoes, chillis, onion and coriander and mix together with the salt and pepper.

Leave the mix to stand for at least 1 hour so that the flavours can develop.

Just before serving scoop the flesh from the avocadoes leaving the skins intact and mash the avocado into the tomato mixture.

To serve, spoon the mix back into the avocado skins, garnish with lemon and accompany with garlic bread.

Roasted Red Pepper and Almond Dip serves 4-6

vegan

contains nuts

3	*red peppers*
6	*cloves garlic (unpeeled)*
4½ tbsp	*olive oil*
2 tbsp	*white wine vinegar*
75g	*ground almonds*
	salt and pepper

Place the peppers and garlic cloves in a baking tray and roast in the oven at gas mark 5 for 10-15 minutes, until the peppers are soft and their skins are starting to blacken.

Pop the garlic cloves out of their skins and pull out the pepper stems and seeds, trying not to lose any of the juice from inside the peppers. Put the juice into a bowl until needed. Remove the skins from the peppers.

Place the peppers, garlic, olive oil and vinegar into a blender and chop until smooth. Add the juice from the peppers and the ground almonds and blend again.

Season to taste.

Serve with herb and onion bread and a wedge of lemon.

Flatcap Mushroom Pate serves 4-6

75g	*margarine*
2	*shallots (finely chopped)*
1	*garlic clove (crushed)*
225g	*flatcap mushrooms (sliced)*
25g	*fresh breadcrumbs*
100g	*cottage cheese*
	pinch of grated nutmeg
	salt and pepper

Melt 25g of margarine and fry shallots and garlic for 3 minutes, until soft.

Add mushrooms, cover and cook for 15 minutes.

Remove pan lid and reduce the liquid by increasing the heat.

When very little liquid remains, add the remaining margarine to the pan.

Allow to cool, then blend the mushrooms and the remaining ingredients until smooth. Add seasoning.

Garnish with grated nutmeg and a slice of lemon and serve with garlic bread.

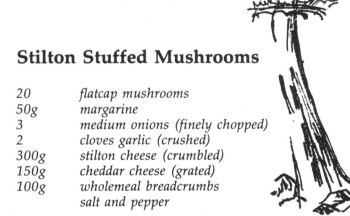

Stilton Stuffed Mushrooms

serves 5

20	flatcap mushrooms
50g	margarine
3	medium onions (finely chopped)
2	cloves garlic (crushed)
300g	stilton cheese (crumbled)
150g	cheddar cheese (grated)
100g	wholemeal breadcrumbs
	salt and pepper

Remove the stalks from the mushrooms and chop the stalks finely.

Fry the onion and garlic in the margarine for 3-4 minutes. Then add the mushroom stalks and cook until they are soft.

Combine the mushroom mix with the cheese and breadcrumbs to form a stiff mixture.

To serve, fill the flatcap mushrooms with the mixture and bake in the oven for about 10 minutes until golden brown.

Falafel with Hot Sauce

serves 4-6
vegan

'When I came to the interview for my job at the Red Herring, they asked me what I liked to cook. When it came to falafel my mind went blank: I think I ended up saying 'oh, I can't remember what they're called, they're those little Middle Eastern thingies made out of chick peas'. They're a good party dish and go well with a moderately hot salsa or a garlicy, lemony, herby yoghurt relish, pitta bread and salad Or try them in sandwiches with chutney and salad – the possibilities are endless.'   *Hannah Rye*

225g	chickpeas (soaked overnight)
2	cloves garlic (crushed)
2	medium onions (finely chopped)
2 tbsp	chopped fresh parsley
1 tsp	ground coriander
1 tsp	ground cumin
½ tsp	turmeric
¼ tsp	cayenne pepper
½ tsp	baking powder
	salt and pepper
	oil for deep frying
sauce:	
400g	tin chopped tomatoes
	juice of 1 lemon
3	cloves garlic (crushed)
1 tbsp	finely chopped fresh parsley
1 tsp	brown sugar
½ tsp	chilli paste
	salt

Drain and rinse the chickpeas then cook in fresh water until soft. When cooked, drain the chickpeas and mash or blend them to a paste.

Add the remaining ingredients and mix thoroughly, then leave to stand for 30 minutes.

Form the mix into 14-16 balls. If they are too sticky roll them in a little plain flour.

Heat the frying oil in a pan, then fry the falafel until brown and crisp. Place on kitchen paper to absorb any excess oil.

To make the sauce, place all the ingredients into a small heavy pan, then bring to the boil. Once boiling, simmer the sauce uncovered over a low heat for 20-30 minutes, stirring frequently.

Check the seasoning of the sauce and leave it to cool.

Serve the falafel hot on a bed of lettuce with a ramekin of the cold sauce. A warm pitta bread makes an ideal accompaniment.

Parsnip and Sweetcorn Fritters   serves 4-6

'It was mind over batter, but the batter got the better of me'
Simon Shields, on making fritters

450g	parsnips (finely chopped)
75g	sweetcorn
batter:	
75g	plain flour
2 tsp	baking powder
1	egg (beaten)
75 ml	milk
1 tsp	margarine
	salt and pepper
	oil for shallow frying

Cook the parsnips until tender, and when cooked, add the sweetcorn.

To make the batter, combine the flour, baking powder, egg, milk, margarine and seasoning. Whisk thoroughly until well mixed.

Combine the parsnip and sweetcorn with the batter and mix well. The mix is now ready to fry.

Heat the oil in a frying pan until hot. Take a tablespoon of the batter and drop it into the hot oil. Fry the fritter until golden brown, turning to cook each side.

Serve hot with a yoghurt dressing.

Mixed Nut Balls

serves 4-6
contains nuts

60g	*ground almonds*
60g	*ground hazelnuts*
60g	*ground walnuts*
75g	*breadcrumbs*
100g	*cheddar cheese (grated)*
1	*egg (beaten)*
75 ml	*sherry*
1	*small onion (finely chopped)*
1 tbsp	*fresh ginger (grated)*
1 tbsp	*chopped fresh parsley*
1	*green chilli (finely chopped)*
1	*red pepper (diced)*
	salt and pepper

Mix the nuts, breadcrumbs and cheese.

Mix the remaining ingredients together and add to the nut mixture. If the mix is too dry, add more sherry, if too wet, add more breadcrumbs.

Shape into 25 mm balls and bake at gas mark 5 for 15-20 minutes until golden brown.

Vegetable Kebabs

serves 6

6	*tomatoes (cut into quarters)*
3	*courgettes (sliced)*
3	*red peppers (halved then each half cut into 4)*
24	*25 mm cubes of mozzarella cheese (optional)*
dressing:	
2 tbsp	*balsamic vinegar*
2 tbsp	*olive oil*
1 tbsp	*finely chopped fresh basil*
1	*pinch mustard powder*
	freshly ground black pepper

Assemble each kebab with 2 quarters of tomato, 2 slices of courgette, 2 pieces of red pepper and 2 cubes of mozzarella.

To make the dressing, combine the vinegar, olive oil, basil and mustard powder and whisk until thoroughly mixed.

Brush the kebabs with the dressing and grind with pepper. Place on a baking tray and bake at gas mark 5 for about 5 minutes until the dressing is sizzling and the mozzarella is slightly melted.

Serve on a bed of green salad, with 2 kebabs per person.

Patlican Tava

serves 4-6

vegan

2	*large aubergines*
	oil
sauce:	
2	*cloves garlic (crushed)*
6	*tomatoes (peeled and chopped)*
1 tbsp	*wine vinegar*
1 tsp	*sugar*
1 tbsp	*currants*
	salt and pepper
6 tbsp	*pine kernels (toasted)*

Slice the aubergines into 5mm thick rounds, salt them and leave to stand for 30 minutes, then wash well in cold water.

Allow the aubergines to drain then place them on a baking tray and brush with a little oil.

Bake the aubergines in a moderate oven for 10-15 minutes, turning them halfway through cooking, until they are soft and slightly browned.

To make the sauce, fry the garlic in oil and then add the tomatoes, vinegar, sugar, currants and seasoning and cook for 3-4 minutes.

To serve, place the warmed aubergine slices on a bed of lettuce and top with the sauce and toasted pine kernels.

Mixed Vegetable Pakoras

serves 4-6
vegan

175g	mushrooms or courgettes (sliced) or cauliflower florets, or a combination of all 3 which gives a more interesting dish
2-3 tbsp	sunflower oil
1 tbsp	black mustard seeds
1	large onion (finely chopped)
2	cloves garlic (crushed)
batter:	
8 tbsp	gram flour
2 tsp	ground cumin
2 tsp	ground coriander
2 tsp	turmeric
3 tsp	garam masala
1½ tsp	baking powder
½ tsp	chilli powder
1 tsp	salt
1 tsp	pepper
	oil for frying

Heat the oil and once hot fry the mustard seeds, stirring occasionally, until they pop.

Reduce the heat and add the onion and garlic and fry until tender. Then add the vegetables and fry for 2-3 minutes. Remove from the heat.

To make the batter, place the gram flour in a large mixing bowl with the cumin, coriander, turmeric, garam masala, baking powder, chilli powder, salt and pepper. Mix well.

Add the fried ingredients to the batter mix. Stir thoroughly to form a stiff binding mixture. A little water may need to be added if the mixture is too dry.

Fry the batter coated vegetable pieces in hot oil until golden brown.

Serve hot on a bed of lettuce with red sauce.

The Cafe Opens

The opening was imminent. We had to plan for it and so my friend Sian offered to organise the opening. Andy and Aidan were up all night baking mountains of good things. I was finishing off various, endless tasks at the cafe. Timmo was sorting out a major problem with the gents toilet, but the tables were standing, the walls were painted, Timmo's Japanese paper corner lights were beautiful, the stove was in, the cooker worked, we had a fridge and water, work surfaces and a counter, plates and glasses, cups and tea pots, forks and spoons, pans from the scrap yard cleaned and sparkling. My dad had given us some lovely knives he had from a lifetime as a cutler in Sheffield.

That morning, it was delightful to go into the cafe and see the builders yard and chaos of the previous days and months transformed into a charming little cafe with crisp white tablecloths on the trestle tables, each with a vase of flowers. I breakfasted there, served and waited on by friends as glad it had come about as I was myself. I was allowed a relaxing breakfast of coffee and croissants before the madness of the day descended.

Then we were running, serving lunches and teas, and awaiting the band in the evening that played and played while people queued on the street for a taste of the atmosphere and food which didn't always come up to scratch or temperature but at least was there on the tables. The fully legitimate Red Herring was open with sign painted and welcoming.

The day before we'd had a great shock when a suited gentleman walked off the street and into our preparations. He said he'd seen a poster advertising the opening and it certainly hadn't come through his office. 'Well, who are you?' I asked. 'The Chief Planning Officer actually'. I explained my approach to his department months before and the outcome of the discussions. He was quite worked up about it, but I showed him around and explained what we'd done and why and how. He left saying, 'Well, it doesn't look like you're going to open tomorrow and you can't have live music because you haven't got a licence but forget I've been here, I've not been here, right?!' I invited him to the opening but he declined and that's the last we heard of it!

The first 'normal' day of the cafe opening was Shrove Tuesday, 1987. I was cooking alone in the cafe and struggling to produce a mountain of pancakes. As has so often happened over the years, someone turned up in the nick of time and gave me a really needed helping hand. Sometimes it all seemed so very unreal, but that was usually strangeness induced by extreme tiredness and overwork. Quite often I

would bake in the morning and then work an evening shift in the cafe. We were always making do with quite inadequate equipment and having to go shopping at least once a day because we couldn't afford to buy more than just enough for one day at a time.

After the cafe had been going some time and had begun to establish itself, we took on the shop as well. Eddie's had struggled and it was inevitable that Steve, its proprietor, would move on. We bought him out. It was not expensive, there was so little stock by the time he finally gave up it only cost £300 or so.

The poster for the opening of the Red Herring in 1987

Main Courses

At the Red Herring we serve main dishes which have their origins in the four corners of the world. There is chiles rellenos, a vegan Latin American dish; briam, a Mediterranean hotpot of delicious vegetables and cheese; aubergine and potato curry, a definite flavour of India; and sweet and sour tofu stir fry, inspired by Chinese cuisine. We also ensure that traditional vegetarian cooking can be sampled in the form of nut roasts, numerous pasta dishes, lasagne and bean casseroles. We have a wide variety of dishes to suit all tastes and all occasions and the following section contains our favourites.

Jenny serving in the shop

Nutty Mushroom and Stilton Crumble
Hazelnuts, mushrooms, leeks and celery in a creamy stilton sauce with a nut and cheese crumble topping.

Nut and Seed Croustade
A layer of toasted nuts and seeds topped with a creamy mixed vegetable sauce and melted cheese.

Lima Bean Crumble
Butter beans, broccoli, mushrooms, leeks and peppers in a creamy sauce topped with nuts and cheese crumble.

Red Dragon Pie
A vegetarian version of shepherd's pie.

Three Cheese Pie
A rich, creamy, cheesey pie with nuts under a puff pastry crust.

Quiche
A pastry case with sliced onions, a combination of cooked vegetables and a savoury egg mix topped with grated cheese and garnished.

Curried vegetable pasties
Filling spicy pasties, delicious hot or cold and ideal for packed lunches and picnics.

Arabian Apple Beanpot
A spicy butterbean and apple casserole served with yoghurt and apricot sauce and garlic bread.

Provencale Bean Stew
The Red Herring's version of the traditional French recipe.

Fasoulia
A Middle Eastern bean casserole.

Chestnut and Winter Vegetable Hotpot
A seasonal dish which is easy to make and full of flavour.

Tempeh and Vegetable Kebabs
These kebabs are so easy to make and delicious served with rich and creamy gado gado sauce.

Sweet and Sour Tofu Stir Fry
This combines crunchy vegetables, delicious tofu and a sweet and sour sauce to create a wonderfully tasty dish.

Greek Style Stuffed Aubergine
Aubergines with a tomato, onion and rice stuffing and baked.

Courgettes Farcies aux Mousserons
Courgettes filled with mushrooms, spinach, cream cheese and pistachio nuts.

Briam
A Mediterranean hotpot of aubergine, pepper, potato, tomato and feta cheese cooked in a generous amount of olive oil and black pepper.

Biber Dolmasi
Middle Eastern style peppers stuffed with rice, pine kernels, currants and fresh herbs.

Indonesian Vegetable Curry
A mild mixed vegetable curry cooked in a sauce of spices and creamed coconut.

Aubergine and Potato Curry
A medium curry, dry in consistency and flavoured with spices and fresh coriander.

Split Pea Dhal
An ideal accompaniment to curry.

Spiced Cashew Rice
A delicious rice dish for serving with any curry. Brown basmati rice flavoured with spices and fresh garlic, chilli and ginger.

Peanut Sambal
A spicy peanut relish to serve with Indonesian vegetable curry.

Toasted Cashew Nut and Red Wine Moussaka
A vegetarian version of this traditional recipe.

Cannelloni
Pasta filled with a rich mixture of tomatoes, herbs, walnuts and red wine and baked in a cheese sauce.

Pasta Tocca di Funghi
Pasta baked in a rich tomato and mushroom sauce and topped with a generous swirl of cream and cheese.

Pasta alla Siracusana
Pasta baked in a sauce of peppers, aubergines and olives and topped with mozzarella cheese.

Mushroom and Lentil Lasagne
The Red Herring's version of everyone's favourite dish.

Three Nut Burgers
Delicious burgers made with toasted nuts, flavoured with herbs.

Blackeye Bean Burgers
These spicy burgers are easy to make and full of flavour.

Bean Koftas
These aduki bean and bulgar wheat patties are full of fresh coriander, mint and parsley giving them their unique flavour.

Stilton Croquettes
A Red Herring favourite these rich croquettes are easy to make.

Mediterranean Roast Vegetables
A simple and wonderful way to cook vegetables to accompany a roast.

Solstice Roast
One of the Red Herring's favourite nut roasts.

White Nut Roast with Herb Stuffing
A special nut roast for Christmas and other festive occasions.

Pancakes
A very simple easy to make dish given great variety by the diversity of possible fillings: spicy aubergine, mushroom and watercress, spinach and feta cheese and tomato and hazelnut, among others.

Greek Bake
Layers of filo pastry topped with spinach, feta and mozzarella cheese, and tomatoes, and baked until golden.

Mushroom, Leek and Wild Rice Parcels
A delicious combination of ingredients, including nuts, wrapped in filo pastry.

Borek
Spinach and feta cheese filo parcels. Boreki are a smaller version, ideal as a starter.

Broccoli and Cheese Strudel
A rich and delicious combination wrapped in crisp flaky filo pastry.

Sweet and Sour Cashew Nut Parcels
Mixed vegetables and nuts in a sweet and sour sauce made into filo parcels.

Chiles Rellenos
A Chilean dish of oven roasted peppers stuffed with refried pinto beans and topped with spicy salsa.

Lentejas Gratinadas
A green lentil and feta cheese bake topped with fried diced potatoes and melted cheese.

Nutty Mushroom and Stilton Crumble

serves 4-6

contains nuts

2 tbsp	oil
6	sticks celery (chopped)
500g	leeks (sliced)
500g	mushrooms (thickly sliced)
3 tbsp	flour
300 ml	water
100g	hazelnuts (roasted and roughly chopped)
200g	stilton (crumbled)
	salt and pepper

savoury crumble topping:

75g	margarine
200g	85% plain flour
100g	mixed pumpkin and sunflower seeds (toasted)
100g	cheddar cheese (grated)
75g	hazelnuts or peanuts (toasted and roughly chopped)

Heat the oil and fry the celery and leek until soft; then add the mushrooms and fry until cooked.

Add the flour and stir thoroughly. Cook for a few minutes, then remove from the heat and gradually stir in the water.

Return to the boil stirring frequently. Add the nuts and stilton and mix until the stilton melts.

Season with a little salt and lots of ground black pepper.

Make the crumble topping: Melt the margarine, then take off the heat.

Mix the flour, seeds, cheddar cheese and nuts in a large bowl.

Stir in the melted margarine to form a crumb like texture. If the mix feels too dry add a little oil to it.

Place the stilton mix in a casserole dish and top with the savoury crumble topping.

Bake at gas mark 5 for 20-30 minutes until the crumble topping is golden brown.

Nut and Seed Croustade

serves 4-6

contains nuts

base:

100g	almonds (roasted)
50g	poppy seeds
100g	cheddar cheese (grated)
100g	breadcrumbs
1 tsp	marjoram
2	cloves garlic (crushed)
2 tbsp	olive oil

topping:

100g	red peppers (sliced)
100g	mushrooms (sliced)
100g	courgettes (sliced)
100g	broccoli (broken into small florets
100g	sweetcorn
1 tbsp	oil
1	onion (chopped)
1	clove garlic (crushed)
1 tbsp	plain flour
pinch	grated nutmeg
150 ml	milk
100 ml	cream
1 tbsp	shoyu
	black pepper
150g	cheddar cheese (grated)

Prepare the base. Chop the almonds fairly coarsely and mix with the poppy seeds, cheese, breadcrumbs, marjoram, garlic and oil to form a crumblike texture.

Prepare the topping. Fry the onion and garlic, then add the pepper, broccoli, mushrooms and finally the courgettes. Cook until the vegetables are tender, then add the sweetcorn.

Sprinkle with the flour and nutmeg and stir in thoroughly. Gradually add the milk and cream, stirring constantly. Season with shoyu and pepper.

Press the crumble base mixture into a casserole dish and bake at gas mark 5 for 5-10 minutes. Remove from the oven and pour the creamy vegetable mixture over the top. Sprinkle with the grated cheddar.

Return to the oven and bake for 15-20 minutes until bubbling and golden.

Lima Bean Crumble

serves 4-6

contains nuts

100g	butter beans (soaked overnight)
50g	margarine
2	small onions (finely chopped)
1	clove garlic (crushed)
200g	leeks (sliced)
150g	mushrooms (cut into quarters)
100g	red pepper (diced)
150g	broccoli florets
50g	plain flour
1 l	milk
2½ tsp	dried tarragon
1 tbsp	shoyu
	salt and pepper
	crumble topping (see previous recipe)

Drain the beans and boil in fresh water until tender but retaining their shape, then drain them.

Fry the onion, garlic and leeks until softened, then add the pepper, mushrooms and broccoli and cook for 5 minutes.

Remove from the heat and stir in the flour, then return to the heat and cook for 1-2 minutes, stirring constantly.

Gradually stir in the milk and then cook until the sauce has thickened, stirring frequently.

Add the tarragon, shoyu, beans and seasoning. Place the mix in a casserole dish and cover with crumble topping.

Bake at gas mark 5 for 20-30 minutes until the crumble topping is golden brown.

Red Dragon Pie

serves 4-6

250g	aduki beans (soaked overnight)
100g	brown rice (soaked overnight)
3 tbsp	oil
2	medium onions (chopped)
600g	carrots (finely diced)
2-3 tbsp	shoyu
2 tbsp	tomato puree
600 ml	stock from the beans
½ tsp	thyme
½ tsp	basil
½ tsp	oregano
½ tsp	dill
	salt and pepper

topping:

500g	swede (peeled and chopped)
500g	potato (peeled and chopped)
1	egg (beaten)
50g	margarine
75g	cheddar cheese (grated)
	salt and pepper

Drain and rinse the beans and rice and then boil them, separately, in fresh water until tender; the beans should retain their shape. Once cooked drain the rice, and then the beans reserving the stock.

Fry the onion and carrot until the carrots are slightly softened. Add the cooked beans and rice.

Mix together the bean stock, shoyu, tomato puree and herbs, then add to the vegetable and bean mix. Stir in well and cook for a further 15 minutes until the carrots are tender. The final mixture should be quite moist. Check the seasoning.

Boil the potato and swede in salted water. When tender, drain and mash. Mix in the egg and margarine and season well.

Put the bean and vegetable mixture in a casserole dish and top with the mashed potato and swede, then sprinkle with the grated cheddar cheese.

Bake at gas mark 5 for 20-30 minutes until the cheese is golden and bubbling.

Three Cheese Pie

serves 4-6
contains nuts

200g	*cream cheese*
6	*eggs (beaten)*
200g	*cheddar cheese (diced)*
200g	*white stilton cheese (diced)*
200g	*broken walnuts (washed)*
2	*onions (chopped)*
2 tbsp	*finely chopped fresh parsley*
	salt and pepper
450g	*pack ready made puff pastry*

Combine the cream cheese and eggs. Add the diced cheeses, nuts, chopped onion and parsley and mix well.

Grease a 230 mm round loose bottomed cake tin and line the base and sides with the pastry, ensuring enough pastry is left for the top.

Pour the pie filling into the tin, then cover with a pastry top. Nip the lid to the pastry around the sides to prevent the mix from leaking. If any pastry remains, use it to decorate the pie.

Bake at gas mark 6 for 45-60 minutes until golden brown.

Quiche

serves 6-8

contains nuts

We make a large, deep well-filled quiche with a variety of fillings. Put a layer of sliced fried onions in a pastry case, add a layer of cooked vegetables, pour on a savoury egg mix, spread with grated cheese and garnish with sliced tomatoes, peppers, mushrooms or with flaked almonds or other nuts and seeds.

450g	pastry made with 85% flour
1	medium onion (sliced and fried)
12	eggs
450g	broccoli florets (steamed)
125g	cheese (grated)
200ml	milk
25g	flaked almonds
½ tsp	dried rosemary
½ tsp	dried thyme
	salt and pepper

Roll out the pastry and line a quiche tin at least 35 mm deep and 300 mm diameter. Crimp it round the edges to increase the depth of the shell, right on the top edge of the tin. Press firmly into the sides of the tin, prick with a fork and chill the pastry case before baking in a hot oven at gas mark 7 for 10 minutes.

When the pastry has been blind baked, spread the fried onions on the base and top with the steamed broccoli.

Break the eggs into a large bowl and whisk vigorously with the milk, salt, pepper, and herbs. Pour the egg mixture over the broccoli and spread the cheese evenly over it. Sprinkle with flaked almonds.

Bake at gas mark 4 for 40 minutes. Check after 20 minutes. When ready the quiche should be golden brown and firm in the middle. If needed, turn the heat down a little and cook till set.

Other filling suggestions:

Fried aubergine, or fried mushroom, with tomato; steamed cauliflower and walnuts; steamed courgettes and red pepper; steamed spinach, blue cheese and almonds; fried leek and whole button mushrooms.

Curried Vegetable Pasties

makes 10
vegan

400g	pastry made with 85% flour
filling:	
450g	yellow split peas or red lentils
4	medium onions (finely chopped)
2	medium carrots (diced)
2	cloves garlic (crushed)
2 tbsp	sunflower oil
2 tsp	ground coriander
2 tsp	ground cumin
1 tsp	turmeric
1 tsp	tandoori masala
½ tsp	salt
½ tsp	ground black pepper

Wash the split peas and put in a pan with 10 mm of water above the peas. Bring to the boil and simmer for 30 minutes. Stir frequently to prevent them sticking to the pan but only add more water if absolutely necessary.

Heat the oil in another pan and add all the other ingredients. Stir over a hot flame until the onions are starting to brown, then turn the heat down and simmer gently.

When the split peas are soft and mushy they can be added to the other ingredients, but if they are at all sloppy sieve the excess water off first. Mix all the ingredients together well and simmer for 5 minutes. Remove from the heat and allow to cool.

When the filling is cool roll out the pastry on a floured board until it is between 2 and 3 mm thick. Cut out 15 cm diameter circles by cutting around a suitable bowl or plate.

Brush the edges of each pastry circle with water and put a large tablespoonful of the filling in the centre of each one. Bring the edges together above the filling, seal with your fingers then crimp the sealed edge between forefingers and thumbs to form a cocks comb.

Place on baking sheets and bake in a hot oven, gas mark 6 for 20 minutes or until the cocks combs are brown and the pastry baked through but lighter in colour.

Arabian Apple Beanpot

serves 4-6

vegan

450g	butter beans (soaked overnight)
2 tbsp	oil
2	onions (sliced)
2	cooking apples (sliced)
1 tsp	turmeric
1 tsp	allspice
1 tsp	cinnamon
	salt and pepper

sauce:
225 ml	natural yoghurt
50g	dried apricots (chopped)

Cook the beans until tender, then drain reserving the stock.

Fry the onion until golden, add the apple, turmeric, allspice and cinnamon and cook until the apple is soft.

Add the beans and enough liquid to make a wet mixture. Season and simmer for 10 minutes.

Mix together the yoghurt and apricots and serve as an accompaniment with garlic bread.

Provencale Bean Stew

serves 4-6

vegan

500g	haricot or flageolet beans (soaked overnight)
3 tbsp	olive oil
3	onions (sliced)
1	large red pepper (sliced)
1	large green pepper (sliced)
3	cloves garlic (crushed)
400g	tin tomatoes (chopped)
2 tbsp	tomato puree
1 tsp	marjoram
2 tsp	herbs de provence
100g	stoned black olives
3 tbsp	chopped fresh parsley

Cook the beans until almost tender; drain reserving the stock.

Heat the oil and fry the onion until soft. Add the garlic and peppers and fry for a few more minutes. Add the tomatoes, tomato puree, herbs, beans and enough bean stock to make the stew sufficiently moist. Season, bring to the boil, cover and simmer until cooked.

Stir in the olives and parsley and serve with garlic bread.

Fasoulia

serves 4-6

vegan

'I first came across fasoulia when a friend, who'd eaten it in the Sudan, cooked up a big pot of it. I hadn't been a vegetarian long and was still adjusting from a meat and two veg diet, so I thought it was amazing, really powerful flavours. A Greek woman once told me it was a typically Greek dish but there are variations of it all around the eastern Mediterranean.'   *Hilary Forrest*

450g	haricot beans (soaked overnight)
200 ml	olive oil
1	bulb garlic (crushed)
2	bay leaves
2 tsp	oregano
4 tbsp	tomato puree
	juice of 2 lemons
	salt and pepper
	raw onion rings to garnish
	fresh parsley to garnish

Cook the beans until tender then drain.

Heat the oil and fry the cooked beans with the garlic and bay leaves for 5 minutes.

Add enough water to cover the beans then mix in the tomato puree; simmer for 5-10 minutes until the ingredients are stewed.

Add the lemon juice and seasoning.

Serve with garlic bread and garnish with raw onion rings and fresh parsley.

Chestnut and Winter Vegetable Hotpot serves 4-6

vegan

150g	*dried chestnuts (soaked overnight)*
250g	*carrots (sliced)*
2	*onions (chopped)*
150g	*mushrooms (sliced through stems)*
250g	*sprouts; courgettes can be used instead*
3 tbsp	*oil*
2 tsp	*mustard (dill mustard is the best)*
2 tsp	*shoyu*
1 tbsp	*finely chopped fresh parsley*
	salt and pepper

Drain and rinse the soaked chestnuts. Cover with fresh water, bring to the boil and then cover and simmer for 20-30 minutes until tender but still keeping their shape. Drain reserving the liquid.

Heat the oil and fry the onion, carrot and mustard until the onion is soft.

Add the shoyu, chestnuts and their liquid and simmer for 10 minutes.

Finally add the mushrooms, sprouts and parsley and cook for 15 minutes until the vegetables are tender.

Season, then serve with garlic bread or a baked potato.

Tempeh and Vegetable Kebabs

serves 4

vegan

2	*blocks tempeh (each cubed into 12)*
6	*tomatoes (quartered)*
4	*courgettes (thickly sliced)*
24	*mushrooms*
	tempeh marinade
	oil

Makes 12 kebabs. Other vegetables can be used, such as peppers.

Marinade the cubed tempeh overnight.

Assemble the kebabs in the following order: courgette, tempeh, tomato, mushroom, tomato, tempeh, courgette.

Brush lightly with oil and grind on black pepper. Bake at gas mark 5 for 15 minutes until the vegetables are browned and tendered. Alternatively they can be barbequed.

Serve on a bed of couscous or rice with gado gado sauce or sweet and sour sauce.

Sweet and Sour Tofu Stir Fry

serves 4-6

vegan

45 ml	oil
220g	block smoked tofu
2	onions (finely sliced)
400g	carrots (cut into thin strips)
100g	broccoli florets
1	red pepper (diced)
1	yellow pepper (diced)
400 ml	vegetable stock
200g	fresh pineapple (cubed)
2	cloves garlic (crushed)
3 tbsp	cider vinegar
3 tbsp	tomato puree
3 tbsp	apple juice
1 tbsp	shoyu
3 tsp	arrowroot or cornflour, mixed to a paste with a bit of the vegetable stock
	salt and pepper

Heat the oil and fry the tofu until crispy, remove from the oil and drain off the excess oil.

Fry the onion in the same oil for 10 minutes until soft, then add the carrot and cook for a further 5 minutes. Add the broccoli and pepper, cook until done, then remove from the heat.

Place all the remaining ingredients in another pan and cook until thickened, stirring frequently.

Pour the sauce over the vegetables and return to the heat, cooking for another 15 minutes.

Finally add the tofu and seasoning and cook for 5 minutes.

Serve immediately with noodles or brown rice.

Greek Style Stuffed Aubergine   serves 4-6

This recipe was inspired by some aubergines I ate in Western Crete where the local cooking still relies heavily on vegetables – where it has not been ousted by the ubiquitous pizza, burgers and chips!   *Matthew Davison*

4	*medium aubergines*
	olive oil
4	*ripe tomatoes (peeled and chopped)*
2	*cloves garlic (crushed)*
½ tsp	*oregano*
1	*bay leaf*
50g	*short-grain rice*
	salt and pepper
175g	*feta cheese*
	juice of ½ a lemon

Preheat oven to gas mark 6.

Cut the aubergines in half lengthwise and make a deep slit in each cut face, taking care not to cut through the skin.

Place the aubergines, cut side down, on an oiled baking tray and bake for 15-20 minutes, until fairly soft but not disintegrating. Remove from oven and allow to cool.

Drop rice into a pan of boiling water.

While the rice is cooking heat a few tablespoons of oil and fry the onion until golden brown. Add the garlic, tomatoes, bayleaf and oregano and leave to simmer.

When the rice is barely cooked (after about 10 minutes) strain and add to the tomato sauce. Cook for a few minutes longer if it is a bit runny. It should be thick but not dry.

Using a sharp knife and a teaspoon, hollow out the aubergines, leaving a shell about 5mm thick.

Chop the aubergine flesh and add to the rice and tomato mixture. Season to taste.

Fill the aubergine shells with the mixture and place in a deep oven dish.

Surround with about 15mm of water, a generous sloosh of olive oil and the lemon juice. Cover with foil and bake at gas mark 6 for 20 minutes.

Remove the foil and top the aubergines with slices of feta cheese. Drizzle with olive oil and bake uncovered for a further 15-20 minutes until the feta is lightly browned.

Lift out of any remaining liquid and serve.

The quantity of olive oil may seem rather vague (and quite large). Use as much as you like – it might be fattening but is very authentic and good for your cholesterol level.

Courgettes Farcies aux Mousserons   serves 4

contains nuts

6	courgettes
50g	margarine
2	shallots (finely chopped)
225g	mushrooms (finely chopped)
225g	spinach (chopped)
225g	cream cheese
2 tbsp	tomato puree
	salt and pepper
2 tsp	honey
2	eggs (beaten)
100g	pistachio nuts (coarsely chopped)

Halve the courgettes and scoop out the flesh. Place the courgette skins in boiling water for 15 minutes to soften them.

Heat the margarine and fry the shallots and garlic for 2 minutes. Add the mushrooms and spinach and cook over a low heat until any excess liquid has evaporated.

Stir in the cream cheese, then the tomato puree. Season and add the honey.

Remove from the heat and mix in the eggs and pistachio nuts.

Fill the hollowed courgettes with the mixture and place in a baking tray. Cover the tray with foil and bake at gas mark 5 for 15 minutes. Remove the foil and cook for a further 5 minutes to brown the mixture in the courgettes.

Briam

serves 4-6

'I first tasted this on the Greek island of Skopelos – there are generally so few dishes suitable for vegetarians that we were very lucky to find a restaurant which served a variety of lush home-made vegetarian dishes. I asked the chef how she made this and made a mental note of it. Using her method all the ingredients are put into the dish raw, and baked in a very slow oven for up to 12 hours – I found this quicker version just as good.' *Jane Becconsall*

340g	*potatoes (unpeeled, sliced thinly into rings)*
1	*large aubergine (sliced thinly into rings)*
1	*onion (sliced thinly into rings)*
2	*cloves garlic (crushed)*
1	*red or green pepper (sliced thinly in half rings)*
340g	*tomatoes (sliced thinly)*
225g	*feta cheese (crumbled; although feta made from sheep's milk is more expensive it gives a better flavour to the dish than that made with cow's milk)*
150 ml	*olive oil*
	a little water

Par boil the potatoes for 5 minutes.

Layer the remaining vegetables with about 2/3 of the feta in a large shallow baking dish, starting with aubergines, onions, half the tomatoes, garlic, and peppers, and drizzling olive oil in between layers.

Layer the potatoes on top and finish off the top layer with the remaining tomatoes and feta cheese.

Follow with another generous drizzle of olive oil and a little water (not more than 2 tbsp) to stop the vegetables from drying out.

Bake, covered in a low to moderate oven, at gas mark 5, for 2–2½ hours. Turn up the oven temperature to gas mark 7 and remove the cover after about 2 hours to ensure potatoes, tomatoes and feta turn a nice golden colour.

Serve on a bed of couscous or rice, or in a bowl with crusty bread to mop up the juices.

Biber Dolmasi

serves 6

Stuffed peppers

vegan

6	red or green peppers (halved and deseeded)
3	large onions (finely chopped)
75 ml	olive oil
150g	pine kernels
300g	short grain rice (soaked overnight)
3 tbsp	currants
½ tbsp	brown sugar
700 ml	water
2 tbsp	finely chopped fresh parsley
2 tbsp	finely chopped fresh mint
75 ml	olive oil
	salt and pepper

Heat the olive oil and fry the onion until golden.

Add the pine kernels and fry for 2-3 minutes.

Drain and wash the rice and add this to the onions. Fry in the oil until the rice becomes translucent.

Add the currants, sugar and seasoning, then the water. Bring to the boil, then cover and simmer over a low heat for 15-20 minutes until the water has been absorbed and the rice is tender. Add more water if necessary.

Stir in the parsley and mint.

Fill the pepper halves with the rice mixture and place them in a fairly deep baking tray. Pour in 125 ml water and the remaining olive oil and cover the tray with foil.

Bake at gas mark 5 for 30 minutes until the peppers are soft.

Serve with tomato and apricot sauce.

Indonesian Vegetable Curry

serves 6-8
vegan
contains nuts

2 tbsp	*oil*
1	*onion (finely chopped)*
2	*chillis (finely chopped)*
1 tsp	*ground coriander*
1 tsp	*ground cumin*
1 tsp	*fresh ginger (grated)*
1 tsp	*turmeric*
75g	*almonds (roughly chopped)*
	salt and pepper
¾ packet	*creamed coconut*
500 ml	*boiling water*
	juice of 1 lemon
1kg	*selected vegetables:*
	potatoes (diced)
	white cabbage (finely sliced)
	cauliflower florets
	broccoli florets
	carrots (cut into strips)
	aubergine (cubed and salted)
	peppers (cut into strips)
	courgettes (sliced)

Heat the oil and fry the onion and spices until the onions are soft. Add the coconut and boiling water and stir over the heat until the coconut is dissolved. Then add the nuts and seasoning.

Add the chosen vegetables one at a time, in order of their hardness and cooking times. Simmer until the vegetables are just tender, taking care not to overcook them.

Add the lemon juice and adjust seasoning.

Serve with spiced cashew nut rice and peanut sambal.

Aubergine and Potato Curry

serves 4-6

vegan

4 tbsp	oil
600g	potatoes (diced)
600g	aubergines (diced)
1 tsp	brown mustard seeds
1 tsp	ground coriander
1 tsp	ground cumin
½ tsp	turmeric
½ tsp	cayenne pepper
3 tbsp	water
2 tbsp	fresh coriander
	salt and pepper

Place the aubergine in a colander, then sprinkle with salt and leave to stand for at least ½ an hour. Rinse well and drain.

Heat the oil and when hot add the mustard seeds. When they start popping add the potato and aubergine and stir for 5 minutes.

Add the spices and seasoning and fry for a few minutes more.

Add the water and cover the pan. Simmer over a low heat until the potato is tender, stirring occasionally and adding more water if the vegetables start to stick to the bottom of the pan.

Once cooked, stir in the fresh coriander.

Serve with rice and gujerati salad.

Split Pea Dhal

serves 4-6
vegan

250g	yellow split peas (well washed)
3	green chillis (finely chopped)
6	cloves garlic (crushed)
2 tsp	fresh ginger (grated)
50g	margarine or vegetable ghee
1 tsp	turmeric
1 tsp	ground coriander
2 tsp	garam masala
1 pinch	cayenne pepper
2	bay leaves
	salt and pepper

Place the split peas in a pan and cover with water. Bring to the boil and scrape off any scum floating on the water. Boil rapidly for 10 minutes, then take off the heat.

Fry the chilli, garlic and ginger in the margarine or ghee for 2-3 minutes, then add the spices and fry for 2 more minutes, stirring frequently to prevent burning.

Add the fried spices to the cooked split peas along with the bay leaves. Cover the pan and simmer on a low heat until the peas disintegrate. Stir frequently to avoid the dhal sticking to the pan bottom. Season to taste.

Spiced Cashew Rice

serves 6-8
vegan
contains nuts

3 tbsp	oil
250g	brown basmati rice
4 tbsp	cashew nuts
1	onion (finely sliced)
1	clove garlic (crushed)
1 tsp	fresh ginger (grated)
1	small chilli (finely chopped)
3/4 tsp	garam masala
1 tsp	salt
400 ml	water

Wash the rice by placing it in a bowl of cold water and rubbing the grains together with your hands. Drain the washed rice and rinse well, then return to the bowl and cover with fresh water. Leave to soak for about 30 minutes before draining.

Heat the oil and fry the cashew nuts for 1 minute, no more or they may burn, then remove them from the oil.

Add the onions and fry for 2-3 minutes, then add the rice, garlic, chilli, garam masala and salt. Stir and fry the rice for 8-10 minutes.

Add the water and simmer for 5 minutes, then cover the rice and leave it over a low heat to cook in the steam. Stir at regular intervals to prevent the rice from sticking to the bottom of the pan.

Remove from the heat once the rice is cooked. If it is too moist cover the pan with a clean tea towel and replace the lid, this will absorb the excess moisture.

Stir in the cashew nuts just before serving.

Peanut Sambal

serves 6-8

vegan

contains nuts

125g	*roasted peanuts or peanut butter*
2	*dried red chillis (finely ground)*
2	*cloves garlic (crushed)*
2 tbsp	*shoyu*
2 tbsp	*white wine vinegar*
2 tbsp	*brown sugar*
200g	*fresh tomatoes (finely chopped)*

Roast the peanuts and blend or chop until a fine texture is achieved.

Add the chilli, garlic, shoyu, vinegar and sugar and mix well.

Chop the tomatoes and add the peanut mix to them, folding in thoroughly.

Serve as a cold relish with Indonesian vegetable curry.

Toasted Cashew Nut and Red Wine Moussaka

serves 4-6

2	large aubergines (thinly sliced and salted) contains nuts
2 tbsp	oil
2	large onions (chopped)
2	cloves garlic (crushed)
250g	mushrooms (sliced)
2	green peppers (diced)
100g	cashew nuts (toasted and roughly chopped)
50g	breadcrumbs
1 tbsp	tomato paste
2 tbsp	chopped fresh basil
1-2 tbsp	shoyu
100 ml	vegetable stock
100 ml	red wine
	salt and pepper

sauce:

50g	flour
500 ml	milk
2	eggs (beaten)
100g	cheddar cheese (grated)
	grated nutmeg

Place the sliced aubergine in a greased baking tray, brush with a little oil and bake at gas mark 5 for 5-10 minutes until the aubergines are soft but not browned.

Heat the oil and gently fry the onion and garlic for 5 minutes, then add the mushroom and pepper and cover and cook for 10 minutes.

Stir in the cashews, breadcrumbs, tomato puree, basil, shoyu, stock and wine, and check the seasoning.

Make the sauce by whisking the flour and milk in a pan on a low heat. Increase the heat once they are mixed and keep stirring until the sauce thickens.

Take off the heat and stir in the beaten eggs and cheese.

Place half the vegetable mixture in a large baking tray. Top with half the aubergines, then another layer of mix and the rest of the aubergines.

Pour the cheese sauce over the top and grate on a little nutmeg.

Cover the dish with foil and bake at gas mark 5 for 30 minutes. Remove the foil and bake a further 5-10 minutes to brown the top.

Cannelloni

serves 4
contains nuts

2 tbsp	olive oil
1	onion (finely chopped)
1	clove garlic (chopped)
200g	fresh tomatoes (chopped)
1 tsp	basil
175g	walnuts (finely chopped)
175g	breadcrumbs
150 ml	red wine
	salt and pepper
12	tubes cannelloni
sauce:	
50g	margarine
50g	plain flour
600 ml	milk
150g	grated cheese

Fry the onion and garlic in oil until well softened, then add the tomatoes and cook until just soft.

Remove from heat and add basil, walnuts, breadcrumbs and wine. Mix well, then allow to cook. Check seasoning.

Using a wide piping nozzle and a large piping bag fill the tubes of cannelloni and place in an earthenware ovenproof dish.

To make the cheese sauce, melt the margarine and add flour to form a roux. Using a whisk gradually add the milk, stirring continually to prevent lumps forming.

Cook over a low heat stirring regularly until the sauce thickens, then remove from the heat and add the cheese.

Pour the sauce over the cannelloni so that they are well covered, then bake for 20-30 minutes on gas mark 5 until the cannelloni are soft.

Pasta Tocca di Funghi

serves 4-6

10 tbsp	*olive oil*
400g	*tin chopped tomatoes*
2 tsp	*sugar*
2 tsp	*salt*
2	*bay leaves*
400g	*mushrooms (finely sliced)*
1	*clove garlic (crushed)*
2 tsp	*marjoram*
	salt and pepper
	pasta to serve 4-6 people
	grated cheese
6 tbsp	*cream*

Heat the oil and add the tomatoes, salt, sugar and bay leaves and cook slowly for 15 minutes, stirring frequently.

Add the mushrooms, garlic, marjoram and pepper. Simmer for 15 minutes, stirring occasionally.

Cook the pasta and add to the sauce. Place in an ovenproof dish, add cream and then sprinkle with grated cheese.

Bake in a moderate oven for 15-20 minutes until the cheese is browned and bubbling.

Pasta alla Siracusana

serves 4-6

2	*small aubergines (cubed and salted)*
3	*red, green and yellow peppers (diced)*
3	*cloves garlic (crushed)*
1	*small chilli (finely chopped)*
400g	*tin chopped tomatoes*
100g	*black olives (stoned and chopped)*
2 tbsp	*capers*
2 tsp	*finely chopped fresh basil*
½ tsp	*dried oregano*
	salt and pepper
	pasta for 4-6
	mozzarella cheese (grated)

Prepare the aubergine, grill or roast the peppers until browned and cut into cubes after removing stalks and seeds.

Heat the oil and fry the garlic and chilli for 1 minute, then add the aubergine and cook until the aubergine is just browning.

Add the tomatoes, peppers, olives, capers, basil, oregano and seasoning and cook for 5 minutes.

Cook the pasta and add to the sauce. Place in an ovenproof dish and top with the mozzarella. Bake in a moderate oven for 15-20 minutes until the cheese is melted and bubbling.

Eleanor sharing a joke in the kitchen.

Mushroom and Lentil Lasagne   serves 8

2 tbsp	olive oil
2	onions (finely chopped)
2	carrots (finely chopped)
2	sticks celery (finely chopped)
400g	mushrooms (chopped)
2	cloves garlic (crushed)
2	bay leaves
200g	brown lentils (washed)
400g	tin chopped tomatoes
100 ml	red wine
1 tbsp	chopped fresh basil
	salt and pepper
300 ml	vegetable stock
	lasagne verde
sauce:	
1 l	milk
100g	plain flour
150g	cheddar cheese (grated)
pinches	nutmeg, cayenne and mustard
	salt and pepper
100g	cheddar cheese (grated)

Heat the oil and fry the onions, carrot and celery until the onion is soft. Add the garlic and bay leaves and fry for 2 more minutes.

Add the lentils, tomatoes and wine, and stock if needed and cook until tender. The mixture should be moist but not too wet.

To make the cheese sauce, place the flour in a bowl and gradually whisk in the milk. Transfer to a pan and heat until the sauce starts to thicken, whisking continuously.

Add the cheddar, spices and seasoning and remove from the heat.

Layer as follows, starting from the bottom: lentil mix, lasagne, cheese sauce, lentil mix, lasagne, cheese sauce, then sprinkle with grated cheese.

Bake at gas mark 5 for 30-40 minutes or until the sheets of lasagne are tender.

Three Nut Burgers

serves 4
vegan
contains nuts

50g	*margarine or oil*
1	*large onion (finely chopped)*
2	*sticks celery (finely chopped)*
100g	*roasted peanuts (chopped)*
125g	*roasted hazelnuts (chopped)*
60g	*roasted cashew nuts (chopped)*
125g	*wholewheat breadcrumbs*
1 tsp	*dried basil*
½ tsp	*dried marjoram*
1½ tbsp	*plain flour*
1½ tsp	*yeast extract*
200 ml	*vegetable stock*
1½ tbsp	*shoyu or tamari soy sauce*
1½ tbsp	*tahini*
	salt and pepper
	oil for frying

Roast the nuts at gas mark 5 for about 8 minutes; it is a good idea to roast the nuts in separate dishes as their roasting times may vary.

Allow the nuts to cool, then rub the hazelnuts to remove their bitter skins. Place the nuts in a blender and chop them until they are fairly fine.

Fry the onion and celery until soft, then add the herbs and flour and cook for a few minutes more.

Dissolve the yeast extract in the stock, then add it to the onion and celery with the shoyu. Cook until the mixture thickens.

Stir in the chopped nuts, breadcrumbs and tahini and mix well, then season.

Divide the mix into eight. Then using a burger press or your hands, shape into burgers.

Fry the burgers in hot oil until golden brown and serve with a roll and tomato and fresh basil sauce.

Blackeye Bean Burgers

serves 4-6
vegan
contains nuts

175g	blackeye beans (soaked overnight)
20 ml	oil
2	medium onions (finely chopped)
2	cloves garlic (crushed)
175g	mushrooms (finely chopped)
100g	crunchy peanut butter
1 tbsp	tahini
100g	breadcrumbs
1 tbsp	shoyu
1 tsp	mustard powder or mustard
½ tsp	cayenne pepper
1 tsp	paprika
½ tsp	garam masala
	salt and pepper

Fry the onion, garlic and spices until soft, then add the mushrooms and cook for 2-3 minutes more. Remove from heat.

Cook the beans until very soft, then drain, reserving the stock, and mash well.

Add the beans to the onion and mushroom mixture, and then add the breadcrumbs and mix well.

Mix together the peanut butter, tahini, shoyu and 50 ml of stock and add this to the mixture. If the consistency is too wet, add breadcrumbs; if too dry, add more stock. Check seasoning and shape into burgers.

Fry each burger over a medium heat in very little oil; too much oil can make them fall apart.

Serve with a spicy or sweet and sour sauce.

Bean Koftas

serves 6-8

Based on a North African recipe

100g	aduki beans (soaked overnight)
100g	bulgar wheat
300 ml	vegetable stock
100g	mushrooms (finely chopped)
1	onion (finely chopped)
2	cloves garlic (crushed)
½ tsp	ground coriander
1 tsp	cumin
2 tsp	paprika
1 tbsp	finely chopped fresh mint
3 tbsp	finely chopped fresh parsley
1 tbsp	finely chopped fresh coriander
1	egg (beaten)
	plain flour to coat the koftas
	oil for shallow frying

Drain the aduki beans and boil in fresh water until tender. Drain the cooked beans.

Place bulgar wheat and stock in a pan and cook for 5 minutes until the wheat soaks up the stock.

Saute the mushrooms, onion and garlic for 10 minutes, then add the spices and cook for a further 2 minutes.

Add the cooked beans and fresh herbs to the onion mix. Then blend or mash until fairly smooth.

Add the egg and blend it into the mix.

Transfer the mix to a bowl and add the bulgar. Leave out any excess liquid or the mix will be too wet.

Shape the mix into flat oval patties and coat them in flour. Fry in hot oil until golden brown.

Serve with a sauce, for example sweet and sour sauce or yoghurt and chive sauce.

Stilton Croquettes

serves 5

25g	margarine
2	large onions (finely chopped)
1	clove garlic (crushed)
2½ tsp	dried thyme
125g	vegetarian stilton (crumbled)
175g	vegetarian cheddar cheese (grated)
275g	wholemeal breadcrumbs
1	egg (beaten)
	salt and pepper
1	egg (beaten)
150g	wholemeal breadcrumbs
	oil for deep frying

Fry the onion and garlic in the margarine until soft, add the thyme, cover and cook a further 5 minutes. Remove from the heat.

In a large bowl mix the cheddar cheese, stilton and breadcrumbs. Add the onion mix to this and stir in the beaten egg and mix thoroughly. Season to taste.

Divide the mixture into 10 and mould into balls. Coat with egg and then roll in breadcrumbs.

Deep fry in hot oil until they are golden brown with a crispy coating.

Serve with yoghurt and tahini sauce.

Mediterranean Roast Vegetables

serves 8

vegan

4	aubergines (sliced into thin rounds)
4	courgettes (sliced into thin rounds)
6	whole cloves garlic
8	firm tomatoes (cut into quarters)
1	green pepper (cut into strips)
1	red pepper (cut into strips)
	olive oil
	salt and black pepper

Salt the aubergines for 10-15 minutes; rinse well in cold water.

Place all the vegetables and whole garlic in a large baking tray. Drizzle olive oil and grind black pepper over the vegetables.

Bake at gas mark 4 or 5. Turn the vegetables after 15 minutes, then cook a further 15-20 minutes until they are tender and slightly browned. If they brown too quickly, cover with foil.

Solstice Roast

serves 4-5

vegan

contains nuts

3 tbsp	oil
2	small onions (finely chopped)
2	cloves garlic (crushed)
4	sticks celery (finely sliced)
2 tbsp	plain flour
250 ml	tomato juice
200g	hazelnuts (roasted and roughly chopped)
200g	breadcrumbs
3	carrots (grated)
1½ tbsp	shoyu
3 tbsp	chopped fresh parsley
2 tbsp	tahini
	salt and pepper

Grease and line a 1 kg loaf tin, greasing also the lining.

Fry the onions until soft, then add the garlic and celery and fry for another 5 minutes.

Sprinkle in the flour and stir thoroughly. Cook for 2 minutes then gradually stir in the tomato juice and cook until thickened.

Remove from the heat and add the remaining ingredients.

Fill the tin with the mix and cover with greased foil. Bake at gas mark 5 for 40 minutes, then remove the foil and cook for a further 10 minutes. To check whether the roast is properly cooked, stick a metal skewer into the centre and if it comes out clean the roast is done.

Serve the roast in slices with red wine sauce, mediterranean roast vegetables and a baked potato.

White Nut Roast with Herb Stuffing

serves 5
vegan
contains nuts

50g	margarine
1	large onion (finely chopped)
1 tsp	dried thyme
1 tbsp	plain flour
300 ml	soya milk
225g	mixed nuts, cashews, almonds and pine kernels (toasted and finely chopped)
100g	white breadcrumbs
	salt and pepper
1-2	pinches freshly grated nutmeg
3-4 tbsp	white breadcrumbs for coating

stuffing:

175g	white breadcrumbs
100g	margarine
4 tbsp	chopped fresh parsley
	zest of ½ a lemon
2 tbsp	grated onion
1 tsp	marjoram
1 tsp	thyme

Grease and line a 1 kg loaf tin.

Melt the margarine and fry the onion until soft. Add the thyme and flour and cook for 2 minutes stirring well. Gradually add the soya milk and stir until thickened.

Take off the heat and add nuts, breadcrumbs, seasoning and nutmeg.

Sprinkle the inside of the lined tin with the remaining breadcrumbs.

Make the stuffing by mixing all the ingredients together.

Spoon half the nut mixture into the base of the tin, cover with the stuffing mixture. Then add the remaining nut mixture. Press well down to compact it.

Cover the tin with foil and bake at gas mark 5 for 1 hour.

Serve in slices with roast parsnips and potatoes, mediterranean vegetables and onion and sherry gravy.

Pancakes

serves 6-8

Batter:
450g	plain flour
pinch	salt
4	eggs (beaten)
900 ml	milk

Whisk together all the ingredients and leave to rest for 30 minutes.

To cook, lightly oil a frying pan. Pour in a little batter and fry on a high heat. When the mix is no longer runny, flip the pancake over and cook the other side.

Spiced aubergine pancake filling

100 ml	oil
700g	aubergines (diced)
1 tsp	fresh ginger (grated)
2	cloves garlic (crushed)
1 tsp	cayenne pepper
2	leeks (sliced)
200 ml	vegetable stock
1 tsp	sugar
2 tbsp	chopped fresh chives
250 ml	soured cream
75 ml	natural yoghurt

Heat the oil and saute the aubergines for 5 minutes, then remove from the pan.

Add the garlic, ginger, cayenne and leeks to the oil and saute for 5 minutes until the leeks are soft.

Add the stock and sugar, and then the cooked aubergine and cook for a further few minutes.

Fill the pancakes with the mixture and either fold them in half to enclose the mix or roll up.

Combine the chives, soured cream and yoghurt and pour over the pancakes just before serving.

Mushroom and watercress pancake filling

50g	*margarine*
1 bunch	*spring onions (finely chopped)*
900g	*mushrooms (finely chopped)*
2	*small bunches watercress (finely chopped)*
	salt and pepper
100g	*cheddar cheese (grated)*

Fry the spring onions in the margarine for 2-3 minutes, then add the mushrooms and cook for 10 minutes more, stirring occasionally.

Remove from the heat and drain the mix to get rid of any excess liquid.

Put the onion and mushroom mix in a bowl and add the watercress. Season to taste.

To serve, roll or fold the mix in the pancakes and sprinkle with grated cheese.

Spinach and feta pancake filling

25g	*margarine*
2	*onions (finely chopped)*
2	*cloves garlic (crushed)*
450g	*spinach*
	juice of ½ a lemon
pinch or 2	*nutmeg*
225g	*feta cheese (cubed)*
	salt and pepper

Melt the margarine and fry the onion and garlic for 10 minutes until soft.

Add the spinach, lemon juice and nutmeg and cook for 10 more minutes.

Remove from the heat, and allow to cool slightly before adding the feta cheese. Check the seasoning.

Roll up the mixture in the pancakes and place them on a lightly greased baking tray. Bake at gas mark 5 for 20 minutes until crispy. Serve with tomato and basil sauce.

Tomato and hazelnut pancake filling   contains nuts

6	tomatoes (chopped)
125g	breadcrumbs
1 tbsp	oil
1	onion (finely chopped)
1	clove garlic (crushed)
100g	hazelnuts (roasted and ground)
½ tsp	thyme
1 tbsp	tomato puree
3 tbsp	red wine
	salt and pepper
½ tsp	honey
sauce:	
3 tbsp	plain flour
300 ml	milk
½ tsp	thyme
1 tsp	dijon mustard
1	bay leaf
100g	cheese (grated)
	salt and pepper

Mix the chopped tomato and breadcrumbs and leave to stand for 10 minutes.

Heat the oil and fry the onion for 10 minutes, then add it to the tomato and bread mixture with the garlic, nuts, thyme, tomato puree, wine, salt and pepper and honey.

To make the sauce, whisk the flour and milk together over a moderate heat until it starts thickening, then add the remaining sauce ingredients.

To serve, fill the pancakes with the mixture and pour the sauce over them.

Making Filo Parcels

The following diagrams show how to assemble filo parcels, there are 2 basic shapes.
1. Cigar or cylindrical.
2. Triangular.

— TO MAKE CIGAR SHAPED PARCELS.

1.

Brush 1 sheet of filo with oil + place another sheet on top. Place a spoonful or two of the mix in the area indicated.

2.
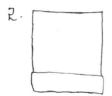

Start to roll the filo, wrapping the mix quite tightly, until 3/4 of the pastry has been used, stop at this point and brush the remaining filo pastry with oil

3.
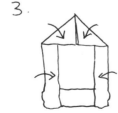

Fold in the vertical edges then the top corners. Continue to roll the filo to form a neat cylindrical parcel.

—TO MAKE TRIANGULAR SHAPED PARCELS.
This method may look more complicated but it
is still relatively easy to do if the method
below is followed.

1. Brush 1 sheet of filo with oil +
    fold it in half. Place a spoonful of
    the mix in the position shown
    then fold corner A over the mix
    to point B to form a triangle of
    filo over the mix.

    B
    A mix

2. Fold the corner C over to point
    D to form another triangle.
    Brush the remaining unfolded
    filo with oil.

    D
    C

3. Fold corner E to point F

    F
    E

4. Fold corner G to point H, then fold
    in the last triangle of filo to
    finish off the parcel.

    H
    G

'Simon Shields, one of my contemporaries at the Red Herring, used to tell me of his 'filo phobia'. Being a bit of an amateur psychologist, I asked him about his childhood, thinking I might find a connection between that and his adult cooking fear! He confessed that he never liked cutting out and sticking, model-making or in fact doing anything fiddly at school. Strangely enough I was the opposite, and sure enough I felt instantly at home working with filo pastry. Simon did, however, overcome his fear and grew to enjoy the wonders of filo!'   *Hannah Rye*

Greek Bake serves 8

1	*packet filo pastry*
	olive oil for frying and brushing pastry
2	*medium onions (chopped)*
4	*cloves garlic (crushed)*
700g	*frozen spinach (defrosted)*
	juice of ½ a lemon
	salt and pepper
200g	*feta cheese (crumbled)*
225g	*mozzarella cheese (grated)*
300g	*fresh tomatoes (sliced)*
75g	*breadcrumbs to coat the tomatoes*

Fry the onion and garlic until soft, then add spinach, lemon juice and seasoning. Cook over a low heat for 10 minutes. If the mixture is too wet, remove the excess liquid by sieving or draining the mixture.

Take a baking tray the same size as a sheet of filo pastry and layer the sheets with a generous brushing of oil between them.

Spoon the spinach mix onto the filo pastry then cover with the crumbled feta cheese, ¾ of the mozzarella and the breaded tomato slices. Sprinkle the remaining mozzarella on top.

Bake at gas mark 6 for 15 minutes until the bake is starting to brown.

Mushroom, Leek and Wild Rice Parcels serves 5

vegan
contains nuts

25g	*soya margarine*
450g	*leeks (chopped)*
450g	*mushrooms (sliced)*
175g	*long grain brown rice (cooked)*
50g	*wild rice (cooked)*
50g	*walnuts (washed)*
1½ tsp	*dried oregano*
4 tbsp	*soy sauce*
	salt and pepper
10	*sheets filo pastry*
	oil
	sesame seeds

Fry the leeks in the margarine until soft, then add the mushrooms and cook for a few more minutes.

Add the cooked rice, walnuts, oregano, soy sauce and seasoning, then allow to cool.

Brush the filo pastry with oil and assemble into triangular parcels. Brush with oil and roll in sesame seeds.

Place on a baking tray and bake at gas mark 5 for about 10 minutes until the filo pastry is golden brown.

Serve with a sauce.

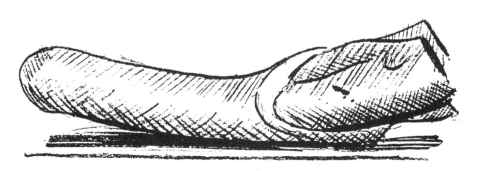

93

Borek

serves 5

	oil for frying
5	onions (chopped)
4	cloves garlic (crushed)
600g	spinach
300g	feta cheese (cubed)
2 tsp	oregano
	juice of 2 lemons
10	sheets filo pastry
	freshly ground black pepper

Fry the onions and garlic until soft, then add the spinach. Ensure that the spinach is not too wet; if it is, drain of the excess liquid.

Remove from the heat and add lemon juice, feta cheese, herbs and pepper.

Assemble into triangular parcels and place on a baking tray.

Bake at gas mark 5 for about 10 minutes until the filo pastry is golden brown.

Serve with a lemon wedge and parsley.

This recipe can also be used to make **boreki**, a smaller parcel which is a lovely starter.

Broccoli and Cheese Strudel

serves 6

50g	margarine
3	onions (finely chopped)
4	heads broccoli (finely chopped)
200g	breadcrumbs
200g	cheddar cheese (grated)
2	eggs (beaten)
	juice of 1 lemon
	salt and pepper
6	sheets filo pastry

Fry the onion in the margarine with a pinch of salt, then add the broccoli and another pinch of salt and cook until soft, stirring frequently.

Add the remaining ingredients and mix well.

Make into cigar shaped parcels and bake on gas mark 5 until browned.

Serve with a sauce.

Sweet and Sour Cashew Nut Parcels   serves 5

vegan

contains nuts

100g	*toasted cashew nuts*
½	*bunch spring onions (chopped)*
5	*sticks celery (chopped)*
3	*peppers (chopped)*
150g	*mushrooms (sliced)*
4	*carrots (chopped)*
4	*cloves garlic (crushed)*
2 tsp	*fresh ginger (chopped)*
1	*large green chilli (chopped)*
½ tbsp	*soy sauce*
½ tbsp	*wine vinegar*
100ml	*pineapple juice*
2 tsp	*sugar*
1 tbsp	*tomato puree*
1 tbsp	*cornflour*
10	*sheets filo pastry*

Fry the vegetables over a high heat, stirring constantly.

Add the chilli, garlic and ginger and fry for a few more minutes. Reduce the heat once cooked.

Mix the soy sauce, vinegar, pineapple juice, sugar and tomato puree and add to the vegetables.

Add a little water or fruit juice to the cornflour and stir to form a paste. Then add this to the vegetables and stir in well, over a low heat until it thickens and coats the vegetables.

Check the seasoning, then assemble into triangular parcels.

Place the parcels on a baking tray and bake at gas mark 5 for 10 minutes until the pastry is golden brown.

Chiles Rellenos

Peppers stuffed with refritos and coriander

serves 6
vegan

6	*green peppers*
refritos:	
300g	*pinto beans (soaked overnight)*
1	*small onion (finely chopped)*
2	*cloves garlic (crushed)*
4 tsp	*oil*
½ tsp	*black pepper*
½ tsp	*salt*
2	*onions (finely chopped)*
2 tbsp	*oil*
4-5 tbsp	*chopped fresh coriander*
2	*green chillis (finely chopped)*
	salsa

Roast the peppers at gas mark 5, turning after 5-10 minutes so that they are evenly cooked. Leave in the oven until the skins are browned.

To make refritos, drain the beans and rinse thoroughly. Place them in a large pan with the onion, garlic and pepper. Cover the beans with cold water and bring to the boil. Once boiling, cover and simmer for 30 minutes, stirring occasionally, until the beans are tender. When cooked, mash the mixture.

Heat a little oil in another pan and pour in the bean mixture, fry it for 5 minutes mashing and stirring continuously to achieve a creamy texture.

In another pan heat more oil and fry the onions until soft. Add the refried beans, coriander and chilli and mix well.

Pull the stalks and seeds from the peppers and stuff them with the bean mixture.

Bake at gas mark 6 for 10-15 minutes and serve with heated salsa sauce on top.

Lentejas Gratinadas

serves 5-6

400g	green lentils (washed)
2 tsp	cumin seeds
3 tbsp	oil
450g	onions (finely sliced)
5	cloves garlic (crushed)
500g	fresh tomatoes (finely diced)
1 tbsp	chopped fresh basil or parsley
½ tsp	oregano
pinch	salt
½ tsp	white pepper
75g	breadcrumbs
200g	feta cheese (crumbled)
400g	potatoes (diced)
	oil for shallow frying
100g	cheddar cheese (grated)

Place the lentils and cumin seeds in a pan and cover with cold water. Bring to the boil and simmer for 25 minutes until soft.

In another pan, heat the oil and fry the onion and garlic until soft. Add the chopped tomatoes with the basil or parsley and cook for 5 minutes. Add the oregano and salt and pepper.

Add the lentils and breadcrumbs to the tomato mix and then the feta cheese. Mix well, the consistency should be thick but not too dry.

Shallow fry the potatoes until golden brown.

Put the lentil mix in a casserole dish, top with the potato and then cover with the grated cheddar.

Bake on gas mark 7 for 5-10 minutes until golden brown.

Sauces and Dressings

So many recipes in this book would be incomplete without an accompaniment. This section provides a range of sauces, gravies, dips and dressings which add the finishing touch. They are all quick and easy, bringing more flavour, colour and texture to a dish.

Accompaniments balance a meal. White nut roast would not be the same without mushroom and sherry gravy and a salad without a dressing would lack flavour and moisture.

It is worth spending a little more time to prepare the accompaniments that make the meal.

Gado Gado Sauce
A spicy Indonesian peanut sauce.

Tomato and Basil Sauce
The basil gives this versatile sauce its unique flavour; it is ideal whenever a sauce is required.

Sweet and Sour Sauce
Delicious with burgers or tempeh kebabs.

Tomato and Apricot Sauce
A rich sweet and sour sauce, ideal with filo dishes.

Red Wine Sauce
A rich sauce for special occasions.

Carrot and Orange Sauce
A sweet sauce for burgers or filo dishes.

Mushroom and Sherry Gravy
Ideal for special occasions, especially a Christmas nut roast.

Raita
A cucumber and yoghurt relish which is served with curries and other dishes of Indian origin.

Tzatziki
A Greek style yoghurt sauce.

Yoghurt and Chive Sauce
Combining yoghurt and fresh herbs gives a good sauce for starters and main dishes, especially falafel and stilton croquettes.

Yoghurt and Tahini Sauce
A rich flavourful yoghurt sauce, ideal with falafel or stilton croquettes.

Vegan mayonnaise
Our vegan version of this popular salad accompaniment.

Creamy Mustard Dressing
A spicy dressing for use with salads or to accompany starters.

Garlic and Herb Vinaigrette
This combines ingredients to give a deliciously distinct flavour.

Tempeh Marinade
Tempeh should always be soaked in this overnight, as this greatly enhances its flavour. The marinade can be kept and used as a sauce.

Spicy Apple and Ginger Chutney
This makes a fine accompaniment to both roasts and curries.

Salsa
Zingy and chunky Latin American sauce to top off a dish. Serve with either chipped potatoes for patatas bravas or tortilla chips for totopos con salsa as a starter with pancakes.

Adele writing the menu beautifully on the blackboard; some of us struggle to be legible!

Gado Gado Sauce

vegan

2 tbsp	oil
1	onion (finely chopped)
1	clove garlic (crushed)
1	bay leaf
1½ tsp	grated fresh ginger
½ tsp	salt
7 tbsp	peanut butter
1 tbsp	honey or brown sugar
	juice of 1 lemon
1 tbsp	white wine vinegar
750 ml	water
2 pinches	cayenne pepper
1 tsp	soy sauce
	salt and pepper

Heat the oil and gently fry onion, garlic, bayleaf and ginger; add the salt during cooking to bring out the flavours and fry until the onion is translucent.

Add the peanut butter, honey or sugar, lemon juice, vinegar, water, cayenne, soy sauce and seasoning and mix thoroughly.

Simmer over a low heat, stirring frequently until the sauce thickens. Cook until the sauce has a thick and creamy consistency.

Tomato and Basil Sauce

vegan

2 tbsp	olive oil
2	large onions (chopped)
1	clove garlic (crushed)
200g	tin chopped tomatoes
150 ml	vegetable stock
2 tsp	dried or fresh basil
½ tsp	oregano
2 tbsp	tomato puree
1 tbsp	concentrated apple juice
	salt and pepper

Fry the onion and garlic in the oil until soft.

Add all the remaining ingredients, bring to the boil and cover. Simmer for 10-15 minutes.

Allow to cool, then blend until smooth.

Season to taste and reheat as necessary.

Sweet and Sour Sauce   vegan

1	onion (chopped)
2 tbsp	oil
1	green pepper (deseeded and finely diced)
1 tbsp	cornflour
½ tsp	ground ginger
½ tsp	mustard powder
275 ml	vegetable stock
2 tbsp	tomato puree
225g	can pineapple pieces (drained)
1 tbsp	wine vinegar
1 tsp	sugar
	salt and pepper

Heat the oil and fry the onion for about 5 minutes, then add the pepper and fry for another 4-5 minutes.

Stir in the cornflour, ginger, mustard, and then gradually add the stock, stirring all the time.

Bring to the boil and stir until thickened, then add the tomato puree.

Roughly chop the pineapple pieces and add them to the sauce with the vinegar and sugar.

Season and simmer gently for 10 minutes to allow the ingredients to combine.

Serve the sauce hot.

Tomato and Apricot Sauce

vegan

	margarine for frying
1	onion (finely chopped)
200g	tin of chopped tomatoes
75g	dried apricots
500 ml	vegetable stock
2 tsp	dried tarragon
1½ tbsp	white wine vinegar

Fry the onion in the margarine for 10 minutes.

Add tomatoes, apricots, stock, tarragon and season with salt and pepper.

Cover and bring to the boil; simmer for 15 minutes.

Remove from heat and stir in the vinegar.

Allow to cool and blend until smooth.

Reheat as necessary.

Red Wine Sauce

vegan

50g	margarine
2	onions (finely chopped)
2 tbsp	plain flour
6	fresh tomatoes (chopped)
¼ bottle	red wine
300 ml	vegetable stock
4 tbsp	chopped fresh parsley
	salt and pepper

Fry the onion until browned, then stir in the flour and allow to cook for 1 minute.

Add the vegetable stock gradually, stirring all the time to avoid lumps.

Add the tomatoes and red wine and simmer covered for 20 minutes. Add the parsley then season to taste.

Carrot and Orange Sauce   vegan

	margarine for frying
1	large onion (finely chopped)
300g	carrots (chopped)
	juice and zest of 1 orange
300 ml	vegetable stock
2 tsp	dried marjoram
	salt and pepper

Fry the onion until soft.

Add all the remaining ingredients.

Bring to the boil, cover and simmer for 15 minutes.

Allow to cool and blend until smooth.

Reheat as necessary.

Mushroom and Sherry Gravy   vegan

	margarine for frying
2	small onions (finely chopped)
125g	mushrooms (finely chopped)
2 tbsp	plain flour
300 ml	vegetable stock
1 tsp	soy sauce or shoyu
1 tsp	cider vinegar
50 ml	sherry
	salt and pepper

Fry the onions until soft, add mushrooms and fry for a further 2 minutes.

Stir in the flour, allow it to cook for about 1 minute, then gradually add the stock, stirring constantly to avoid lumps.

Add shoyu and vinegar and stir in well. Cook for 10-15 minutes until the sauce has thickened, stirring to avoid lumps.

Stir in the sherry and season.

Raita

250 ml	natural yoghurt
6 tbsp	cucumber (peeled and grated)
1 tbsp	chopped fresh mint
1/4 tsp	ground roasted cumin seeds
	pinch cayenne pepper
1/2 tsp	salt
	black pepper

Combine all ingredients and mix thoroughly.

Chill until required.

Tzatziki

A Greek style yoghurt sauce.

125g	natural yoghurt or Greek yoghurt
1	clove garlic (crushed)
1 tbsp	chopped fresh mint
125g	cucumber (peeled, grated and squeezed dry)

Combine all the ingredients.

Allow to stand at least 30 minutes to let flavours develop.

Yoghurt and Chive Sauce

250 ml	natural yoghurt
3 tsp	lemon juice
2 tbsp	fresh chives (finely chopped)
	pinch of paprika
	salt and pepper

Combine all the ingredients, chill until needed.

The chives can be replaced by fresh mint for a yoghurt and mint dressing.

Yoghurt and Tahini Sauce

1½ cups *light tahini*
1½ cups *natural yoghurt*
1   *clove garlic (crushed)*
½   *cup lemon juice*
¼   *cup spring onions (finely chopped)*
¼   *cup finely chopped fresh parsley*
1   *pinch paprika*
½ tsp   *ground cumin*

Mix together all the ingredients.

Season to taste

Vegan Mayonnaise   vegan

175 ml   *soya milk*
1   *garlic clove (crushed)*
         rind and juice of ½ a lemon
         pinch of salt
1 tsp   *mustard*
350 ml   *olive oil*

Blend soya milk, garlic, lemon and salt.

Gradually blend in the olive oil.

Chill until firm.

Creamy Mustard Dressing   vegan

2 tbsp   *dijon mustard*
75 ml   *any white vinegar*
150 ml   *olive oil*
1 tsp   *cayenne pepper*
         salt and pepper

Combine all the ingredients and whisk well.

Garlic and Herb Vinaigrette

2	*cloves garlic (crushed)*
5 tbsp	*olive oil*
2½ tbsp	*red wine vinegar*
	pinch of celery salt
¼ tsp	*mustard powder*
¼ tsp	*dried dill*
¼ tsp	*oregano*
¼ tsp	*dried basil*
1 tbsp	*lemon or orange juice*
	salt and pepper

Combine all the ingredients and mix well.

If stored in a tightly sealed container the vinaigrette will keep for a long time.

Tempeh Marinade   vegan

This marinade is one that can be used for any dishes involving tempeh. The tempeh should be left in the marinade overnight so that the flavours are well absorbed.

2	*blocks tempeh (cubed)*
4	*cloves garlic (crushed)*
2	*green chillis (chopped)*
2 tsp	*fresh ginger (chopped)*
1	*small cinnamon stick*
1	*pinch of nutmeg*
100 ml	*shoyu*
	boiling water

Combine all the ingredients in a large bowl.

Add the cubed tempeh and enough boiling water to cover the tempeh.

After removing the tempeh the marinade can be blended and used in a sauce.

Spicy Apple and Ginger Chutney vegan

225g	cooking apples (peeled, cored and diced)
225g	onions (chopped)
70g	sultanas
100g	soft dark brown sugar
100 ml	wine vinegar or cyder vinegar
2 tsp	fresh ginger (grated)
2	pinches salt
1	pinch cayenne pepper

Place all the ingredients in a heavy bottomed pan and bring to the boil.

Simmer uncovered over a low heat for 1-1½ hours stirring occasionally.

When the consistency of the chutney is thick and no excess liquid appears when it is parted with a spoon it is properly cooked.

Cool well before serving.

Salsa vegan

1	onion (roughly chopped)
2	cloves garlic (crushed)
2	chillis (finely chopped)
1	large red pepper (roughly chopped)
4 tbsp	chopped fresh coriander
1 tbsp	tomato puree
500g	tomatoes (chopped)
	salt and pepper

Fry the onion and chillies in oil until soft, then add the remaining ingredients and stew until the pepper is tender.

Season to taste.

Edible Flowers

'At age five I was fascinated by a particularly large clump of velvety red snapdragons in my parents' garden. Convinced they'd melt in my mouth and taste of sweet cinnamon, I managed to resist for several weeks. I even stole stems to offer my teacher. I still remember spitting out the horrible flower and the acute disappointment!

These days I feel like a vindicated child. When bright red, yellow and orange nasturtiums arrive in the summer to be tossed into the Red Herring's green salad, I can hardly wait. The sweet, peppery taste of those blooms in my mouth, fulfilling their sunshiny promise and almost making up for that snapdragon.

In June 1996 I made an unusual wedding cake for friends who are organic gardeners: dark chocolate cake flavoured with rosewater and covered in fresh edible flowers. It caused a sensation, particularly with the children at the reception. I told them to ask their parents before plundering their gardens at home . . . I didn't recommend snapdragons.

In case you're as enthusiastic as me and them, here is a list of edible flowers. Some go well in salads, some are good for garnishing desserts, and some have little taste but look pretty. Don't get your flowers to eat from florists, who grow them for appearance, not taste, and spray them. Organic ones from your own garden are best. The Red Herring's edible flowers are grown at Bradley Gardens, near Ryton and are ordered through Mill Herbs.'   *Nichole Messier*

Violas, violets and pansies – delicate and sweet, leaves edible too.
Rose or lemon geranium – smell heavenly.
Cowslips and primulas – look pretty, little taste.
Pink rosepetals – taste as they smell. Enhance their flavour with rosewater. Rosepetal sorbet and crustless little sandwiches of bread, butter and pink rosepetals were popular with Victorian ladies. For some reason red ones aren't considered edible.
Carnations – taste spicy. White wine stuffed with carnation petals, left overnight and strained off, is an exotic drink.
Marigolds (or calendula) – taste of tarragon and decorate temples in India. Dried petals can be used as a colouring agent like saffron.
Lavender – another old-fashioned favourite. Has been used to flavour stews, beverages and jellies.
Hollyhocks – slightly sweet and delicate.
Courgette flowers – can be stuffed with a flavoured cream cheese mixture for a stunning, simple starter.
Borage – blue flowers that taste of cucumber. Folklore says it gives courage.

Nasturtiums – taste somewhat like watercress. Both leaves and flowers are edible. Capers are pickled nasturtium buds. Not suitable for garnishing sweets.

Chamomile – looks a bit like daisies, tastes of apple. Chamomile tea helps digestion and soothes both children and adults.

Flowers of herbs – garlic, chives, sage, basil, mint and marjoram flowers make interesting savoury garnishes.

Red clover – grows wild and is slightly sweet and spicy.

Heather – looks pretty but is a bit woody. The Picts made ale with heather, not hops, and needed to add no sugar because it contains so much sweet nectar.

Hawthorn flowers – nicknamed 'bread and cheese'. Taste of not much but look pretty.

Elderflowers – another hedgerow flower, with a sweet musky taste. Don't use the bitter stems. Gather the flowers when they're creamy, not white and starting to smell too pungent. If you can't be bothered making elderflower champagne, buy elderflower cordial and make it with fizzy water. Float a few flowers on it to impress your friends.

Elderflower fritters are made by dipping a spray of the flowers into pancake batter and snipping the batter-coated flowers from their stems as they fry.

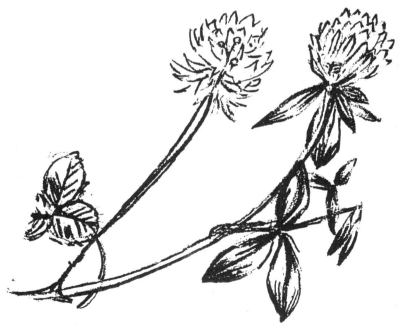

Sprouts for Salads

Take a humble seed, bean or grain and sprout it, and you've just multiplied the goodness it can offer you. You could live (quite cheaply) on sprouts alone, if you ate several kinds together. Sprouts contain amino acids, essential fatty acids, natural sugars and a high vitamin and mineral count. Humans have been eating sprouts for nearly 5000 years; Chinese manuscripts from 2939 BC mention them. The Himalayan Hunzas, famous for their long lives and health, eat sprouts. Beans contain something called phytic acid that prevents some of their nutrients from being used by the human body; sprouting them neutralises it.

Take charge of growing your own organic food, without needing an allotment: grow some sprouts! All you need is a clean jar, some water, some seeds, a sieve or cheesecloth, and a windowsill. It's a great way to show children that food is a process, not something found in a supermarket.

Try sprouting alfalfa seeds, mung beans, chickpeas, aduki beans, whole grains like oats or wheat, and lentils of any sort. Do NOT sprout kidney beans, which are poisonous when raw.

How to do it

You will end up with eight to ten times the volume of sprouts from the seeds you use.

Put a handful of beans, seeds or whole grains in a jar. Cover them with water and soak them overnight.

Pour off the soak water, either draining the seeds in a sieve, or through cheesecloth fastened over the jar's mouth with an elastic band. Rinse the seeds in fresh water and drain off the excess so they don't rot. Don't seal the jar; they need air.

Repeat the rinsing and draining every day to keep them damp. In hot weather you may need to do this up to three times a day.

Keep your sprouts in a warm dark place between rinsings.

After three to five days they will be nearly ready. Put them on a bright windowsill to green up for a few hours in the sunshine.

Put them into the best salad you've ever had! Try to eat them within a week, after which their nutritional intensity begins to decline quickly.

Salads

Salads are often seen as being unique to the summer time. This however is a view which is not held at the Red Herring, where salads are served as accompaniments to many of our main dishes right through the year.

Salads provide us with the perfect opportunity to be experimental; so many different ingredients can be combined to create a cornucopia of tastes.

Crunchy vegetables, fruits, nuts, seeds, beans, fresh herbs and dressings can all be combined to produce a great variety of delicious salads. There are no rules which makes salads an area of cooking creativity.

As with soups, the Red Herring salads are always vegan but cheeses, yoghurt and non vegan dressings can be easily incorporated into recipes to given even greater variety.

It is important to remember that salads are often seasonal. Because fresh fruit and vegetables are major ingredients some recipes are more suited to particular seasons when the fruits and vegetables are widely available and at their very best.

'Salad making can be incredibly satisfying. A salad is a very versatile thing; it can be a quick snack, a whole meal or even a work of art, as well as just being an accompaniment. It can also be highly nutritious, with the addition of fresh herbs, toasted nuts and seeds. Salad-making at the Red Herring had its advantages and disadvantages. The advantage was that almost everything you could possibly wish to put in a salad was to be found there. The disadvantage was that you had to make it by the bucketful!' *Hannah Rye*

Chilean Salad
A signature Red Herring salad, distinctively flavoured with fresh coriander.

Cabbage Salad
A far cry from a simple coleslaw, this salad is full of flavours and colours and the crunchy vegetables and nuts give it a delicious texture.

Brussels Sprouts and Carrot Salad
Although sprouts are not generally seen as vegetables suited to a salad this recipe certainly dispels the myth.

Chickpea Salad
Vivid yellow colour and rich flavour make this one of our most popular salads.

Sprouted Chickpea Salad
A deliciously crunchy salad with a sweet nutty flavour.

Waldorf Salad
The Red Herring's version of this popular salad, the red apples and black grapes make it colourful and sweet.

Rice Salad
Yellow turmeric rice, fresh vegetables, dried fruit and nuts make this salad so colourful and full of flavours.

Gujerati Salad
A delicious carrot salad which is an ideal accompaniment to curry dishes.

Tabbouleh
A middle eastern bulgar wheat salad which derives its unique taste from fresh herbs and a tangy dressing.

Three Bean Salad
A fresh tasting, hearty classic.

Potato Salad
A variation on the traditional potato salad, it uses a vinaigrette rather than mayonnaise.

Butterbean and Fresh Fennel Salad
Fresh fennel gives this salad its unique taste.

Red and Yellow Salad
Red peppers, carrot and sweetcorn give this salad its name; a mixture of crunchy fresh vegetables in a deliciously tangy dressing.

Courgette and Carrot Salad
A crunchy salad with nuts and seeds.

Chilean Salad

serves 4-6

vegan

250g	firm tomatoes (sliced into rounds)
250g	red onions (sliced into rings)
3-4 tbsp	chopped fresh coriander

dressing:

4 tbsp	olive oil
4 tbsp	lemon juice
2 tbsp	red wine vinegar
	salt and pepper

Place the sliced onion and tomato in a large bowl.

Combine dressing ingredients and mix well.

Add to the onion and tomato and stir in the chopped coriander.

Season to taste.

Cabbage Salad

serves 4-6

vegan

contains nuts

225g	red cabbage (finely chopped)
100g	white cabbage (finely chopped)
1	red pepper (cut into thin strips)
50g	toasted sunflower seeds
100g	salted peanuts
50g	raisins

dressing:

1 tbsp	wine vinegar
2 tsp	mustard
6 tbsp	oil
1 tbsp	chopped fresh parsley
	salt and pepper

Combine the salad ingredients.

Whisk the dressing ingredients and add to the cabbage and mix thoroughly.

Brussels Sprouts and Carrot Salad

serves 4-6

vegan

450g	Brussels sprouts (washed and thinly sliced)
3	carrots (grated)
3 tbsp	sultanas
1	small onion (finely chopped)
dressing:	
6 tbsp	oil
2 tbsp	wine vinegar
2 tsp	sugar
3 tsp	dijon mustard
	salt and pepper

Combine sprouts, carrots, sultanas and onions in a bowl.

Mix dressing ingredients and add to the salad, ensuring there is sufficient dressing to make the salad moist.

Check seasoning and chill for at least 1 hour before serving.

Chickpea Salad

serves 4-6

vegan

250g	chickpeas (soaked overnight)
2	courgettes (finely diced)
1	red pepper (finely diced)
3 tbsp	chopped fresh coriander or chives
dressing:	
80 ml	oil
	juice of 2 lemons
2 tsp	turmeric
2 tsp	fresh grated ginger
2	cloves garlic (crushed)
½ tsp	fresh chilli or chilli sauce
	salt and pepper

Cook the chickpeas until tender.

Combine the dressing ingredients and add to the chickpeas while they are still warm, so that they absorb the liquid.

Allow to cool, then add courgettes, red pepper, fresh coriander or chives and salt and pepper.

Sprouted Chickpea Salad

serves 4-6

vegan

This is a wonderful crisp salad, good to make at any time of year. The sprouted chickpeas have a sweet nutty flavour. Sprouting also increases the amount of vitamins and minerals in the beans.

250g	chickpeas
1	green pepper (diced)
1	red pepper (diced)
1	bunch spring onions (finely chopped)
	vinaigrette style dressing

Wash the chickpeas and soak in plenty of cold water overnight. Drain them then place in a container with a loosely fitted lid. Put the container in a warm dark place, such as an airing cupboard, which will promote sprouting.

For the next 3 days, the chickpeas need to be rinsed every morning and evening. They will start to grow small shoots. When these shoots reach 1 cm in length they are ready. Give them a final rinse and refrigerate until needed.

Chop the peppers and spring onions, make the vinaigrette and mix these with the sprouted chickpeas.

Waldorf Salad

serves 4-6

vegan

contains nuts

4	sticks celery (chopped)
3	red eating apples (sliced)
100g	seedless grapes
50g	walnuts (washed)
1	small head of cauliflower (optional) (cut into florets)
	vegan mayonnaise
	juice of 1 lemon

Toss the apple slices in the lemon juice to prevent them browning.

Combine celery, apples, grapes, walnuts and cauliflower (if using).

Add sufficient mayonnaise to coat the ingredients and mix well.

Rice Salad

serves 4-6

vegan

contains nuts

225g	*organic long grain rice (washed)*
2-3 tsp	*turmeric*
2	*courgettes (finely sliced)*
1	*red pepper (diced)*
1	*green pepper (diced)*
50g	*garden peas*
50g	*toasted red skin peanuts*
50g	*currants*
dressing:	
6 tbsp	*oil*
3 tbsp	*vinegar*
1½ tsp	*mustard*
	salt and pepper
	pinch of sugar

Put the rice and turmeric in a pan, add twice as much water as rice, bring to the boil and simmer until the rice is tender.

Drain, rinse and leave to cool.

Add courgettes, peppers, peas, nuts and currants to the rice.

Combine the dressing ingredients and whisk well.

Add the dressing to the rice and stir it all thoroughly.

Gujerati Salad

serves 4-6

vegan

500g	*carrots (peeled and coarsely grated)*
½ tsp	*salt*
	zest and juice of 1 lemon
50 ml	*oil*
1½ tbsp	*whole black mustard seeds*

Mix grated carrot and salt.

Heat the oil until very hot and add the mustard seeds. When the seeds start to pop, take off the heat and pour over the carrot.

Add lemon juice and rind and stir well.

Tabbouleh

serves 6-8

vegan

200g	*bulgar wheat*
1 tsp	*salt*
300 ml	*water (boiling)*
dressing:	
50 ml	*olive oil*
50 ml	*lemon juice*
2 tbsp	*chopped fresh mint*
1-2	*cloves garlic (crushed)*
5 tbsp	*chopped fresh parsley*
6	*firm tomatoes (chopped)*
½	*cucumber (sliced)*

Mix bulgar wheat and salt, add the boiling water and stir well.

Allow to stand for 15 minutes until the wheat is swollen and the water is absorbed. Leave to cool.

Mix the dressing ingredients and pour over the wheat.

Fold in the tomato and cucumber.

Tabbouleh should be served a day after being made so that the flavours are enhanced.

Three Bean Salad

serves 6-8

vegan

200g	*red kidney beans (soaked overnight)*
200g	*chickpeas (soaked overnight)*
200g	*butterbeans (soaked overnight)*
4	*firm tomatoes (quartered)*
4-5 tbsp	*chopped fresh chives*
	french dressing
	juice of 1 lemon

Cook the beans, in separate pans as they have different cooking times. Do not overcook. Drain and wash the beans until cool.

Add the tomatoes, chives, dressing and lemon juice and mix well to ensure that the dressing coats the beans.

Potato Salad

serves 4-6
vegan

300g	*potatoes (scrubbed and cut into chunks)*
1	*bunch spring onions (finely chopped)*
1	*green pepper (diced)*
1	*red pepper (diced)*
150g	*sweetcorn*
2 tbsp	*finely chopped fresh mint*
2 tbsp	*finely chopped fresh chives*
2 tbsp	*black mustard seeds*
dressing:	
6 tbsp	*sunflower oil*
	juice of 1 lemon
2 tbsp	*wine vinegar*
1 tsp	*mustard powder*
	salt and pepper

Boil the potatoes until just tender; do not overcook. Drain them and rinse in cold water to prevent the ptoatoes from continuing to cook.

In a large bowl, combine the potato, spring onions, peppers, sweetcorn, fresh herbs and mustard seeds.

To make the dressing, whisk all the ingredients together.

Pour the dressing over the potatoes and stir in well.

Season with salt and pepper.

Butterbean and Fresh Fennel Salad

serves 4-6
vegan

200g	*butterbeans (soaked overnight)*
200g	*fresh fennel (finely chopped)*
2	*red peppers (diced)*
	vegan mayonnaise
3 tbsp	*apple juice*
	salt and pepper

Cook the beans until tender, drain and allow to cool.

Mix beans, fennel and peppers together. Add mayonnaise and apple juice; mix thoroughly. Season to taste.

Red and Yellow Salad

serves 4-6

vegan

contains nuts

4	sticks celery (finely chopped)
1	small head of cauliflower (broken into florets)
2	red peppers (diced)
4	small carrots (diced)
200g	sweetcorn
50g	walnuts (washed)

dressing:

4 tbsp	olive oil
2 tbsp	red wine vinegar
2 tbsp	tomato puree
2 tsp	chilli sauce
1	clove garlic (crushed)
½ tsp	brown sugar
	salt and pepper

Place all vegetables in a large bowl and add the walnuts.

Combine dressing ingredients and whisk well.

Add the dressing to the vegetables and mix thoroughly.

Courgette and Carrot Salad

serves 4-6

vegan

contains nuts

350g	carrots (coarsely grated)
200g	courgettes (coarsely grated)
500g	toasted red skin peanuts
50g	toasted pumpkin seeds
3 tbsp	black poppy seeds
50g	sesame seeds
	french dressing

Prepare the carrots and courgettes and add the toasted nuts and seeds.

Add the dressing to the salad and mix well.

Baking Bread

I had never or rarely baked bread until after the summer I spent at the Village Bakery in Melmerby in 1982. I came back to Newcastle with a 32 kg sack of 100% organic wholemeal flour from the Watermill in Little Salkeld, and started making bread.

Dough is simple and forgiving. Don't be daunted by it. Make bread and make it again. If you can't work out what the problem is, try another recipe, a different flour, another type of yeast, until you have something you like. If you're using a tin, the consistency is not so critical. You can often get away with a very sloppy dough. Without a tin it has to have enough structural integrity to support itself during the rising process, not collapsing or spreading. The bread with the hole in the middle is most frustrating. Normally its cause is too weak flour – that is, flour with a low gluten content – which is made into a too dry dough. Dry dough can also yield a crumbly bread which dries out quickly.

I have had my fair share of sad and bad loaves. Simply by repeating the process regularly you will get better at it. Baking bread reveals a state of mind, so if you're feeling good, good bread comes easily and if you're anxious, perhaps less so. Nevertheless making bread is a very therapeutic activity.

Get into the kneading, just do it. Be with the dough, roll with it, don't think about anything else. Just be the dough, be one of the ingredients, merge with the flour and water . . . You are the active ingredient, as important as the leaven, as significant as the salt. You and the dough are a culmination of so many things which formed the soil which grew the grain to make the flour. You ate bread to make bread. It is a simple, unifying, transformative process. Those unremarkable ingredients are brought together in a bowl to become something most of us love to share.

Once you have developed a little confidence it will take remarkably little preparation time. Most of the time will be in waiting for the dough to rise and then bake. You can be doing all sorts of things, like making a pizza topping for that bit of dough left over and rising nicely, waiting to be spread with something lush before being baked off.

For most things we prefer a hottish oven. In my experience all ovens vary, so get to know your own oven and only use the recommendations in the recipe as a guide. When you become confident you can vary aspects of most recipes to make them more to your taste, pocket or available ingredients. *Nigel Wild*

Nigel rolling out bread rolls.

Rolls

You can make rolls with all the doughs described, but make sure the dough is nice and soft.

The herb and onion dough makes great rolls for veggie burgers. Try just dipping them in flour, or roll into a sausage shape and tie a simple knot in them first. To tie the knot make a loop in the sausage and stick one end through the loop. Dunk in soya milk or dip in flour.

White rolls are nice knotted in the same way, dunked in soya milk and then in poppy or sesame seeds.

Brown Bread

makes 4 loaves
vegan

1350g	100% organic flour
25g	yeast
2 tbsp	oil
10g	sea salt
	warm water

The Watermill's stoneground organic English flour generally works very well, depending on the harvest or batch of grain at the mill. It imparts a nutty flavour and a fairly dense texture. The gluten content is not as high as some other flours. These days we use half Watermill and half Doves Farm 100% wholemeal organic flours and find the combination provides a close textured flavoursome loaf which is rarely crumbly or with holes. The Doves Farm flour has a guaranteed gluten content.

Traditionally it is recommended that the yeast is mixed with sugar and warm water an hour before baking to start the yeast fermenting. In the bakery and at home I just mix all the ingredients together in a bowl until a soft dough is formed. When all the flour and water is combined in one lump I remove it from the bowl and knead it, dusted with a little flour so it does not stick to the bench.

Knead with a rolling motion, leaning on the dough, rocking back and forth as if rolling the dough up. When it becomes long, I turn it round the other way and roll it up again, moving it all the while. Whichever way you do it, just work the dough, move it, pull it, stretch it. What you are doing is developing the gluten in the bread. This is an elastic protein element which will allow the bread to rise without collapsing. The yeast releases carbon dioxide as it metabolises within the dough, feeding off the carbohydrate in the flour. The elastic strands of gluten trap bubbles of CO_2, causing the dough to rise.

After a good knead, which may be 5 or 15 minutes, depending on how vigorous you are and whether you are enjoying yourself, you can put the dough straight into an oiled tin or on a greased tray, moulded into an attractive shape. Before leaving it to rise in a warm and draught-free place, brush the top with water, soya milk, milk or oil to prevent it drying out as it is rising.

Rising will probably take half an hour. The dough should be somewhere between 1½ times to twice its original size. When suitably risen put in a hot pre-heated oven at gas mark 6. It is best to put it in the oven as it is still rising, to finish doing so in the oven in the moments before the heat kills the yeast. At the peak of its rising you risk a potential collapse of the risen dough in the oven.

Check the bread after about 15 minutes and adjust the temperature if it is browning too quickly. A batch of small loaves should be ready in 30 minutes in a hot oven while larger loaves take 45 minutes at a slightly lower temperature. Ensure large loaves are baked right the way through. Tap the bottom of the loaves and if you get a good hollow response you can be fairly confident it is well baked.

This method allows the dough to rise only once in the tins. You can let it rise once in the bowl, before giving a second kneading and placing it in the tins or on trays.

Read the above instructions and you can apply the general principle and that basic recipe to most flours. You may need to adjust the volume of water but otherwise it should more-or-less work out. You can make this recipe with 85% wholemeal flour for a slightly lighter loaf.

Special Seed Bread

2250g	*dough made with 85% flour*
100g	*soya flour*
100g	*sesame seeds*
75g	*sunflower seeds*
50g	*pumpkin seeds*
2 tbsp	*water*
	extra sesame, sunflower and pumpkin seeds

Combine the soya flour, weighed seeds and water, then knead into the dough. Form into 5 loaves, brush with soya milk and roll in a mixture of seeds before placing in tins, seed side up.

Allow to rise, then bake at gas mark 6 for 30 minutes.

White Bread

makes 5 loaves
vegan

Use the preceeding recipe with unbleached white flour. We recommend a second rising to maximise development of the gluten which is generally higher in white dough. We don't put our white loaves in tins nor do we brush with soya milk, just roll the moulded dough in white flour and place on greased trays. This gives a pleasing floury finish to the bread.

We make a large batch of white dough and we use it for a variety of breads, for wrapping the Peruvian empanadas and making roliolios. So we take a lump to add to the ingredients for herb and onion bread. Alternatively you can add the herbs and cooked onions at the initial mixing stage of the white bread recipe. Allow for two risings to ensure the loaf ends up soft and well risen.

Herb and onion bread

2250g	*white dough*
2	*medium onions (coarsely chopped)*
	sunflower oil
4 tsp	*dried parsley*
2 tsp	*dried thyme*
	a little flour

Fry the onions in oil until cooked. Then put in a bowl, add the herbs and a little flour and mix to a paste.

Then add the dough and a little more flour to produce a soft but not sticky dough. Knead well so all the ingredients are evenly dispersed through the dough.

Cut into 5 lumps and mould into cylinders twice as long as wide. Place on a greased tray and brush with soya milk, water, milk or egg. Slash several times with a knife to a depth of 1 cm across the width; this produces a pleasing pattern when risen and baked.

Allow to rise until 1½ times or twice its original size and bake in a hot pre-heated oven at gas mark 6 until done.

Dried tomato and pesto bread

2250g	white dough
100g	dried tomatoes
1 tbsp	sunflower or olive oil
2 tbsp	pesto
	salt and pepper

Soak the dried tomatoes covered in water with a tablespoon of oil, preferably overnight. When softened mash in a pestle or mortar or give a quick spin in a liquidiser. The aim is to break up the tomatoes a little but not completely. If they are well pulverised they impart a lovely colour to the dough.

Add the tomatoes and pesto to 225g white flour and mix to a paste with a little sea salt and ground black pepper. Add a little more flour if it is too sticky. Add to the white dough and knead thoroughly until the tomato and pesto paste is evenly mixed in.

Form into 5 spheres, place on greased trays and brush with soya milk, water or egg. Slash with a cross on the top of each loaf and allow to rise.

Bake at gas mark 5 to ensure the soft dough is evenly baked. They will probably need 45 minutes but check after 15 minutes. When baked brush again with soya milk, milk or egg, which gives them a softness and a pleasing glaze.

Olive and walnut bread   contains nuts

2250g	white dough
225g	black Kalamata olives
150g	walnuts
200g	white flour

Stone, chop and slightly mash the olives and mix with the walnuts and flour. Knead into the white dough. If the olives are well mashed and kneaded in thoroughly the dough will develop a lovely purple colour.

Allow to rise for about ½ hour, then give another quick knead. Divide into 5 and mould into cylinders and put in oiled tins. Brush the tops with soya milk and leave to rise again.

Bake in a pre-heated oven at gas mark 6 for up to 45 minutes. Brush with soya milk again to glaze when they have been baked.

Pizza

serves 4

Essentially a pizza is a bread dough topped with a tomato sauce and cheese. You can work endlessly around this theme.

450g	*dough (white or brown or speciality)*
½ l	*tomato pizza sauce*
450g	*cheddar cheese (grated)*
225g	*mushrooms (sliced)*
225g	*olives*
1	*green or red pepper (finely sliced)*
	olive oil or sunflower oil

Roll out the dough and place on a greased baking tray 30 cm x 36 cm. Stretch the dough to fit.

For round pizzas divide the dough into four equal pieces. Make into spheres and roll into circles 20 cm in diameter.

Brush with oil and allow to rise for 30 minutes.

When risen, spread the pizza sauce evenly on the dough, then distribute the cheese and garnish with the mushrooms, olives and pepper.

Bake in a hot oven, gas mark 6, for 30 minutes.

Pizza Sauce

400g	*tin chopped tomatoes*
50g	*double concentrated tomato puree*
1	*small carrot (grated)*
2	*medium onions (finely sliced)*
2	*cloves garlic (crushed)*
2 tbsp	*olive oil*
1 tbsp	*dried oregano*
½ tsp	*dried basil*
½ tsp	*sea salt*
	ground black pepper

Heat the oil in a thick bottomed pan and add the onions, carrot, basil, oregano, salt and pepper. Stir well. When the onions are beginning to brown add the garlic and keep stirring for 2 minutes. Add the tomatoes and tomato puree and stir well.

Turn down the heat and simmer for ten minutes.

Roliolios

makes 4-6

These are a pizza masquerading as a danish pastry.

450g	*white dough*
1	*medium onion (finely chopped)*
3	*tomatoes (finely chopped)*
100g	*cheese (grated)*
½ tsp	*paprika*
	salt and pepper
1 tbsp	*olive oil or sunflower oil*

Fry the onions and tomatoes over a hot flame in a small thick based pan. Add the paprika, a pinch of salt and a sprinkling of ground pepper. Cook until the onions are browning and the tomato is collapsed and becoming sauce. Take off the heat and allow to cool.

Once the sauce is fairly cool roll out the dough into a rectangle, twice as long as wide.

Spread the sauce to within 10 mm of each edge. You can spread the grated cheese on top of the sauce or leave to sprinkle on the top once the roliolios are rising on the baking sheet.

Roll the dough up like a swiss roll. Brush the edge you are rolling towards with milk and seal against the dough as it is rolled up.

Cut into slices and place these flat down on a greased baking tray. Sprinkle cheese on top of each one, if you haven't put it all inside with the sauce.

Allow to rise for approximately 30 minutes in a warm place.

When risen place in a hot oven on gas mark 6 for 20-30 minutes. The cheese should be melted and browning by this time and the dough should be baked but moist.

Peruvian Empanadas

'We discovered these in Peru on the road to Macchu Picchu, when we visited Victor and Maria, old companeros from the Red Herring Workers' Co-op, in 1992. We found Panadero Juan in a courtyard in Pissac tending his wood-fired stone oven. As we arrived these delicacies were coming out of the oven. We devoured the first two, then gorged ourselves on several more. These pasties are covered in white dough rather than conventional pastry. A bagful of Panadero Juan's empanadas, a few coca leaves and you could fly to Macchu Picchu; they are an offering fit for Paccha Mama, the earth goddess of the Andes.' *Nigel Wild*

900g	*white dough*
225g	*spinach (steamed)*
450g	*onions (finely chopped)*
450g	*tomatoes (quartered)*
225g	*feta cheese (crumbled)*
2 tbsp	*oil*
1	*pinch sea salt*
½ tsp	*ground black pepper*
½ tsp	*nutmeg*
1 tsp	*paprika*
4 tbsp	*chopped fresh basil*

Cook the onions, salt, pepper, nutmeg and paprika in the oil. Add the tomatoes, then turn off the heat and mix in the drained spinach. Allow to cool, then gently stir in the feta cheese.

Roll out the white dough about 3 mm thick. Cut out circles about 150 mm in diameter, using a suitable sized bowl or plate to cut around. In the bakery we use a large empty tomato tin as a cutter.

Strain the cooled filling if it is too moist. Place a heaped tablespoon of filling in the centre of a circle of dough. Fold one side over so the edges meet; press together firmly with a fork.

Place the empanadas on oiled baking trays and brush with milk, soya milk, egg or oil and leave them to rise for a while.

Bake in a pre-heated oven at gas mark 6 for 20-30 minutes or until golden brown.

When they come out of the oven brush them again with milk, soya milk, egg or oil to soften and enhance the appearance.

If you want to make vegan ones, replace the feta cheese with chopped walnuts, or try something else like smoked tofu.

Croissants, pizza, granary loaves and roliolios cooling in the rising room.

Croissants

makes 22

900g	*unbleached white flour*
450g	*85% flour*
25g	*yeast*
75g	*soft brown sugar*
	pinch salt
	cold water
350g	*butter*

Mix all the ingredients except the butter into a firmish dough. Knead well and leave to rest for at least 20 minutes. Leave the butter somewhere warm so it is soft and easy to spread.

Roll out the dough on a floured board to form a rectangle 50 cm x 30 cm. Spread butter on the left hand two-thirds, leaving a margin of 10 mm at the edge. Fold the unbuttered third over onto the middle buttered third, then the remaining third onto the others. Pinch the edges together and seal the butter in, using fingers and the rolling pin.

Roll it out again to the same dimensions, keeping it as even as possible. Fold it up in the same way but without adding the butter. Do the same once more. Altogether folded three times, no more.

Rest it in the fridge for 20 minutes or so.

Make a template for cutting out your croissants. Cut an isosceles triangle from a piece of cardboard, with the base 14 cm and 17 cm from the base to the pinnacle.

Roll out the chill dough on a well-floured bench into a longer rectangle, seven widths of template base long by two lengths of template high, or about 95 cm x 34 cm.

Cut around your template. Then roll the triangles of dough from their base to the pinnacle, putting pressure only on the two outer corners, leaving the middle untouched and fat. Curve.

Place on baking trays and brush with beaten egg. Leave to rise for 30 minutes or until 1½ times their original size.

Bake at gas mark 6 or 7 for 15-20 minutes, until golden brown.

Pain au chocolat or pain amande

Cut croissant dough into strips, not triangles, and roll up with pieces of your favourite chocolate or pieces of marzipan.

Hot Cross Buns

makes 12

vegan

'One a penny, two a penny, hot cross buns! If only. I love them: fresh they're gorgeous, but toasted the next day for breakfast, a rare treat!' *Nigel*

900g	*flour, unbleached white, or half white and half 85%*
225g	*sultanas*
100g	*sugar*
25g	*yeast*
1	*pinch salt*
2 tsp	*cinnamon*
1 tsp	*nutmeg*
2 tsp	*mixed spice*
	warm water, or soya milk to enrich the flavour

Mix the ingredients and knead to a soft dough. Knead well then leave to rise for half an hour or so.

Give the dough another kneading. Then divide into two lumps and each lump into six pieces. Roll these into spheres and place on a greased tray. Brush with water, oil or soya milk.

Pipe on the crosses after the buns have risen and just before they go into the oven.

Cross mixture

100g	*white flour*
½ tsp	*baking powder*
150 ml	*water*

Mix the ingredients very thoroughly, ensuring there are no lumps.

Pipe on to the buns using a piping bag and a small round nozzle. Or use a small plastic bag with one corner cut off to give a small hole. This should be enough to enable you to pipe on a thin line of the mixture with full control.

Nigel taking seed loaves from their tins.

'Curried vegetable pasties are simple and wholesome, easy to make and eat and very cheap. I love making them, it's so tactile, squeezing and crimping the edges together. I love the bright yellow and orange of the filling and its spicyness, and I love their shape, like little boats. A tray of symmetrically placed pasties about to be slid into the oven is a magnificent sight. And when I've eaten a pasty and salad, I feel I've eaten well.'
Meg Clarke

Mike and Jenny able to laugh: it's almost breakfast time!

Photo: Mary Rea

Building the Bakery

The bakery oven is the seed which grew into the Red Herring Workers' Co-operative of today. I decided to build it in the backyard of the large Victorian terraced house I shared. The bakery was in our house kitchen (or the house kitchen was becoming a bakery). The larder became the rising room. Racks of bread cooling and the constant opening and closing of the oven door raised the temperature to encourage dough to rise.

The first bread was supplied to Eddie's Wholefoods on Saturday, 4th October 1985. It was made in the gas oven as the coke oven wasn't quite ready. I remember getting £6 for those few loaves, and from it I bought ingredients for the following Tuesday when I was next to deliver. It continued in that hand to mouth manner for a long time. It would have been nice to have reasonable supplies of dried fruit, cocoa, butter, yeast, all those essentials, but there were always improvements to make, equipment to acquire or replace, and decoration to do.

As with the original anarchic Red Herring I was philosophical. I felt that if it was meant to be then we would continue somehow and perhaps even survive an environmental health officer's visit. We tried hard but we just didn't have much money.

A major step was to create a separate kitchen for the house. I would be up for hours baking before the household would emerge for breakfast. I'd try to make space for them while I continued making pasties or croissants. They were remarkably tolerant and supportive considering this inconvenience followed months of banging and dirt from building the oven. Free run of the bakery without the need for domestic consideration brought improvements: tiling the bakery all round up to shoulder height, adding shelves. It was a long, slow process.

We built up a base of loyal customers, such as Mandala Wholefoods, then a workers' co-op. They were very supportive and it was difficult to tell them we wouldn't be supplying any more. We continued supplying the unique and uniquely enthusiastic Henry's Wholefoods mobile shop until the incomparable Henry left to run a bakery himself in Newcastle, New South Wales, Australia. When the cafe opened, I thought it would be much more sensible to just supply our own shop and cafe with a hand cart.

The bakery remains an important element in the Co-op, providing us with a range of products mainly using organic flours.
Nigel Wild

A page from Meg Clarke's notebook detailing how to build a beehive oven from a few bricks and some clay.

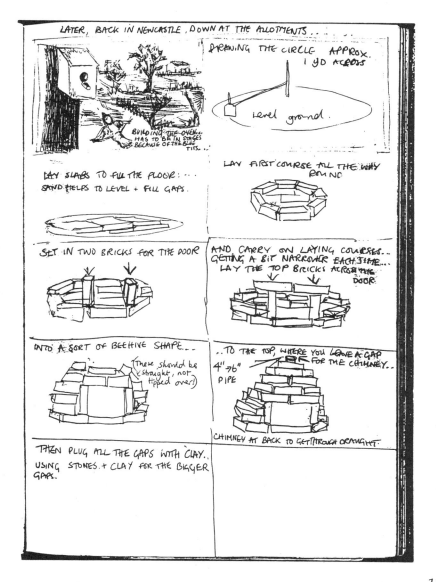

LATER, BACK IN NEWCASTLE, DOWN AT THE ALLOTMENTS...

BUILDING THE OVEN... HAS TO BE IN STAGES BECAUSE OF THE BLUE TITS...

DRAWING THE CIRCLE APPROX. 1 YD ACROSS

level ground.

LAY SLABS TO FILL THE FLOOR:... SAND HELPS TO LEVEL + FILL GAPS.

LAY FIRST COURSE ALL THE WAY ROUND

SET IN TWO BRICKS FOR THE DOOR

AND CARRY ON LAYING COURSES... GETTING A BIT NARROWER EACH TIME... LAY THE TOP BRICKS ACROSS THE DOOR

INTO A SORT OF BEEHIVE SHAPE...

(These should be straight, not tipped over!)

..TO THE TOP, WHERE YOU LEAVE A GAP FOR THE CHIMNEY..

4" TO 6" PIPE

CHIMNEY AT BACK TO GET THROUGH DRAUGHT.

THEN PLUG ALL THE GAPS WITH CLAY. USING STONES + CLAY FOR THE BIGGER GAPS.

'I built my first (and only) oven as a bakery demonstration for the Rising Sun Countryside Centre's open day. My flatmate offered to help and we spent Friday afternoon balancing bricks and stopping all the holes with clay straight from the ground (hence 'mud oven'). You can tell where the gaps are by lighting a little fire inside, and watching where the smoke comes out.

The day of the Open Day was chilly and I was glad to be near the fire, but it was very difficult to get any dough to rise in the wind: I put lots of yeast in, to help it on its way. We chopped pallets for fuel – these ovens need lots because the more heat is retained in the bricks the better they will bake. A fire is lit inside and stoked with dry wood until it's a roaring blaze, then continually stoked until the bread is ready to bake. As quickly as possible the fire is raked completey out. The loaves are then slid in and the door stopped with bricks and sealed with left over dough stuffed in all the cracks. This has the advantage of acting as a timer; when the dough around the door is done, the bread inside will be baked too. We made some edible bread that day, and sold it with butter on, all warm and melting, and sold out very quickly!' *Meg Clarke*

Rachel putting a loaf in the oven we built at Felldyke School, Gateshead.

Photo: Nigel Wild

Eleanor and Adele getting the food and beverages out.

Building the Oven

When I first suggested building an oven in my backyard a lot of people thought it bizarre or mad. I knew nothing of firebricks or lime mortar, about arches or flues or chrome-iron fire-bars. But I put everything into the project – every last penny, all my creative wit and all the strength and determination I could muster. Basically, the idea is to get a box hot enough to bake in and to be able to control and maintain its temperature.

The obvious site was the area previously occupied by the house's privy and coalhouse. What finally emerged after nine months gestation was something akin to Roman central heating. A rectangular box with firebrick walls was capped with two huge stone paving slabs. A firebox at the back heated it from underneath. The whole thing is insulated.

The temperature is controlled crudely by the amount of coke and the speed it burns. The air channel beneath the firebox is totally or partially blocked with a brick, or left fully out for maximum combustion, and a simple push-pull damper regulates the size of the flue opening. We still check the temperature with the back of the hand against the insulated oven door. Can't touch it at all = too hot, while a couple of seconds = too cool.

The oven has served us well with surprisingly little maintenance over the years, except for the grate. At first I used all sorts of things – strange castings recovered from the beach, grates made with very old iron security bars held in cast ceramic retaining blocks . . . One grate now lasts about a year rather than a few weeks. Chrome-iron firebars are clamped at the back and free at the front end to expand and move without too much distortion. The problem used to be getting the oven hot enough; now, with better fuel, it's keeping it down to a reasonable baking temperature!

For the test firing we were very excited and chopped lots of kindling. We put a match to a small pile. There was virtually no draw on the chimney. Smoke came out of the window frames, finding its way into the wall cavities and then escaping wherever possible! The flue we'd used had been blocked. We had to re-route it into the main kitchen chimney. The second firing was a success. I put a wooden door on the oven, stoked the fire furiously and rang some friends to invite them to a celebratory pizza party. It took a long time but eventually the pizza more or less baked; in time to be followed by about a hundred thousand more to date! *Nigel Wild*

Becoming a Co-op

About a year after the cafe had opened a number of people who worked there expressed an interest in becoming a workers' co-op. I had always wanted to be part of a co-op, so we made inquiries. We registered as a workers' co-operative, and five of the original seven were eligible for the Enterprise Allowance. This brought the Co-op a very useful small weekly subsidy for the first year.

The business I ran officially as a sole trader had to cease for thirteen weeks before we could re-open as a co-op and be eligible for the Enterprise Allowance payments. I continued baking to survive, supplying Wholefood Henry. We moved the shop to an underused back room, to provide more cafe seating. We decorated and tiled, made new racks and shelves, bought new crockery and chairs and lots of new tables. We also put a lot of work into the bakery so we could take the bold step of inviting the environmental health officer to visit!

I was nervous. But when she came, she was very considerate of our poverty and I think genuinely impressed that we had done a lot to make it as clean and tidy as possible. She also visited the cafe and we were generally approved of there too. It was a green light, a major achievement.

Several of the members lent the new co-op money. Mostly I brought it the debts I had incurred to get set up. But there was a bakery and a cafe, a fair bit of equipment and fittings and stock and an enormous amount of good will. Those early days of the Co-op were full of lows and highs. Involvement with the Nicaraguan Solidarity Campaign made us aware of the possibilities and importance of international solidarity. It was such a struggle to survive, we were all physically exhausted and anxious about our perilous financial position but there was a strong feeling of comradeship. Sometimes we still feel we exploit ourselves more than anyone else would ever get away with doing. We'd like to pay a decent wage; we'd like everyone to have a decent wage. But we have some say in how we work. This celebration of ten years is an acknowledgement and collective thank you to all who have worked here and made sacrifices for us or on our behalf. *Nigel Wild*

Companera Maria, author of *Food out of Chile*, in the shop before she returned to Santiago in 1990. Meg Clarke, who sent us this photo, said this was exactly how she was standing the first time she saw her.

The Red Herring workers, September 1996:
back row, left to right: Nigel Wild, Nichole Messier, Eleanor Rogers, Jo Ackerman, Jenny Jones;
front row, left to right: Mike Toyn, Adele Sherif, Steve Ridd.

Victor and Maria

Maria and Victor were exiles from the fascist coup d'etat in Chile. It took three years before they arrived in Newcastle in 1976, via Peru, Cuba and Portugal. When I got the oven going Victor asked me to provide pizza for their large Nicaraguan Solidarity Campaign events. I asked if they would like to use the Red Herring on Sundays for a Latin American cafe. Eventually, we asked them to become a part of the Co-op whilst still, if they wanted, running the Sundays themselves. Their maturity and willingness to work very hard made them an important part of the Red Herring. It was five days a week for 'el co-operativo' and then Sunday's event plus a weekly co-op meeting. Madness!

Their return to Chile was momentous. We sent them off by emulating the events at St. Thomas' church which they had organised for so many years. The well respected Bolivian band 'Awatinas' was booked over six months in advance. Twelve weeks before the farewell concert we had the idea for a book to bring together Maria's Latin American recipes and some of the story of their lives. The October 4th concert became a book launch. Miraculously, everything came together and *Food out of Chile* was received from the binders on the very day of the concert. It was a delicious experience opening the boxes full of crisp new books.

The cafe and shop had been shut for the day to prepare. The church was decorated with photographs and aspilleras (political patchworks). A friend of ours, Mark, had spent days making a massive, impressive backdrop. The local band 'Syncopace' very kindly supported 'Awatinas' that night. We expected about 400 people, like Victor and Maria's other concerts; we had 800. There were queues around the church. It was a wonderful event with splendid music, dancing and some very heartfelt speeches. It raised £2,000 for them. All the profit accruing to the Red Herring from *Food out of Chile* has been sent to Victor and Maria over the years. With other generous contributions we were able to send about £5,000 up to now.

I had the great privilege and pleasure of visiting Victor and Maria two years after their return. We took them $7,000 in cash and boxes and bundles of tools for Maria's women's woodwork classes. At the time they were fairly optimistic. Now they are struggling to keep their shop going. It seems unfair.

The Nicaraguan Solidarity Campaign maintained the tradition of Latin American Sundays as long as they could. But they, unfortunately, had to come to an end when a spate of closely co-ordinated pregnancies, reduced (and increased!) their activists. *Nigel Wild*

Poster to publicise the farewell concert in 1990 for Victor and Maria, a night to remember!

From the Cheviots to the Andes
A Farewell Concert for Victor & Maria

AWATIÑAS

TRADITIONAL MUSIC FROM THE BOLIVIAN ANDES

plus the best of Northumbrian music from
FAMOUS SPECIAL GUESTS!!!

and the launch of Maria's book
FOOD OUT OF CHILE
Co-published by Earthright Publications & Red Herring Workers' Co-op

THURSDAY 4th OCTOBER at 7.00 p.m.
St Thomas' Church, St Mary's Place, Newcastle

LOTS OF FOOD!

Tickets £4.50 & £2.50 On door or from the Red Herring (272 3484)

Nichole's lovely festive poster for Christmas 1995.

RED HERRING WORKERS' CO-OPERATIVE LTD.

Special Christmas Menu

During the month of December, the cooks of the Red Herring will be busy creating some wonderfully festive dishes to mark the season, and to share some goodwill and cheer with all of you.

'Sometimes I think we must had been mad. I remember Nigel, Jinny and I catered for a wedding party of 70, three courses. Nigel was a guest, leaving the two of us to silver-serve the whole thing – no-one seemed very keen on helping themselves! Everyone was very patient though and seemed to enjoy the food.'   *Matthew Davison*

Feasts and Festivals

There are always special occasions which require more elaborate and sumptuous dishes. Christmas, birthdays, celebrating and entertaining are all events where eating plays a major role. Because of this, it should be seen as a time to create those dishes which are luxurious, rich in wonderful ingredients and impressive to look at.

Exotic fruits, unusual vegetables, cream, cheeses, herbs, spices and alcohol can be combined with contrasting flavours, colours and components to produce dishes which are ideal for any feast or festival.

Because the recipes are more complicated they do require longer preparation times than most of the dishes in this book. It is a good idea to plan the menu in advance so that ingredients can be bought if needed, and preparation can also begin before the day of the event. Breadcrumbs, pastry and soups can be made and then frozen or refrigerated until needed, pates and cold desserts can be made the day before so that they can be properly chilled. The best way to ensure that all goes right on the night is to try out the more complicated recipes before they are served to guests. This eliminates the possibility of under-estimating preparation times which can lead to recipes being rushed and mistakes being made.

A vegan winter feast

Borscht
Mixed vegetable pakoras
White nut roast with herb stuffing
and tomato and apricot sauce
Apple, almond, date and cyder strudel

A vegan summer special

Spicy garlic and almond dip
Butterbean and fresh fennel salad
Tempeh and vegetable kebabs
with sweet and sour sauce
Summer pudding

A festive winter menu

Pumpkin and ginger soup
Stilton and walnut dip with pears
Mushroom, leek and wild rice parcels
with mushroom and sherry gravy
Chestnut and chocolate pudding

A summer celebration

Tapenade
Chilean salad
Mushroom and watercress pancakes
with yoghurt and chive sauce
Cranachan

Red Herring Christmas Cake

makes 1 cake
vegan

50g	undyed cherries
50g	currants
50g	sultanas
75g	dried apricots (chopped)
75g	dates (chopped)
225 ml	apple juice
200g	100% wholemeal flour
25g	soya flour
1 tsp	bicarbonate of soda
1 tsp	cinnamon
½ tsp	nutmeg
¼ tsp	ginger
75g	soft Muscovado sugar
100 ml	sunflower oil
	juice of ½ a lemon
2 tbsp	apricot jam
	brandy

Soak the fruit overnight in apple juice.

Grease and line with greased greaseproof paper a 20 cm cake tin.

Mix together the flour, soya flour, bicarbonate of soda, spices and sugar. Mix together the oil, lemon juice and jam and stir this into the flour. Then add the soaked fruit. Beat well to blend it.

Pour into the prepared tin and tie a brown paper collar, 50 mm higher than the tin, around the outside with twine.

Bake in a pre-heated oven at gas mark 2 for 1½ hours. Stick a skewer into the centre to see if it is done.

When cool, wrap in cling film and mature for at least 2 weeks, or 3 months. Sprinkle generously with brandy at least once a week.

Meg's Hysterical Christmas

'It was Christmas time 1990 at the Red Herring; the walls were decorated with holly, the bookings diary was full, and a special Christmas menu of delicious complexity had been devised, to run alongside the ordinary menu, and be cooked to order as requested: the central feature, mushroom and stilton pies, had been devised by Matthew, I think. The filling was a tasty mushroom sauce; the stilton was added in generous chunks and the pastry tops rolled out as an order came in; they were then baked in the cafe oven and served fresh with vegetables – gorgeous!

I was the newest member of the Co-op at the time, just picking up on the pace, and that night the pace was extreme. Two large parties of 22 and 15 people had booked and arrived, and several other groups and couples were already in. Victor had to run round to borrow Nigel's kitchen chairs, and the place was so packed that customers had to come to the kitchen door to order and pay their bills, as it was impossible to get to the counter: it was heaving! In the kitchen Victor, Matthew and I were working like galley slaves to get the orders out, when a young couple who had previously booked, came in to order the Christmas menu dishes. This was Matthew's job and he duly went to the end of the kitchen to prepare the pastry etc. leaving Victor and I to keep things going; we were knee deep in piles of washing up by this time, but there was no possibility of doing anything about that, we just had to keep serving.

I was starting to feel overwhelmed, and on the verge of tears, but Victor just kept going and I kept in touch, just . . . until Matthew proudly served his pies with a flourish, only to realise as his customers started tucking in, that he had forgotten to put in any stilton. He was starting to feel the tension too, and when he came back into the kitchen to announce the awful fact (shouting over the uproar of voices and music) he started to hit himself on the head with his rolling pin, he was so cross and wound up . . . and when I saw him, something inside me snapped and I started to laugh and cry simultaneously and uncontrollably: I couldn't stay in the kitchen, and there was nowhere else to go in the building (we had a party dining in the shop too) except the stores cupboard. So I crouched in there among the sacks of beans, tears streaming down my face. Nigel appeared from somewhere and put his head round the door to ask if I was alright and I couldn't answer. I think Nigel helped out in the kitchen until I was able to return: it was only then that I had the brandy, as a restorative and very necessary measure!

Meg Clarke

'I first got involved with the Red Herring working on Sundays with Victor and Maria. That was quite bewildering – working in a kitchen full of people all speaking Spanish, but though I learned my way around the kitchen and gained a very detailed vocabulary of Spanish words for food, it wasn't really much of a preparation for working as part of the Co-op, because everything was on a much smaller scale and much more ad hoc, like selling things you'd made in your own kitchen, which most of the stuff was, on a Saturday afternoon at Victor and Maria's house in Throckley. That's where I first learnt to make empanadas and the process bore no relation to the bakery mass production version. I feel really lucky to have been able to work with Victor and Maria.'   *Hilary*

Greetings from Chile

'One crucial part of our life led us to the north east of England. At that time our origins in the southern hemisphere seemed so far away. However, we set ourselves the fundamental task of not forgetting or becoming alienated from our roots and surroundings and letting others know more about our continent by establishing strong links between both worlds. Hence, the founding of the Red Herring Workers' Co-operative Ltd proved to be one of the most envigorating and important experiences we faced, strengthening this social commitment we felt.

In our opinion, some of the Red Herring's most outstanding achievements have been food and health awareness, the introduction of recipes from all corners of the world and, last but not least, local, national and international solidarity with a social emphasis. Despite all the inevitable difficulties we faced and the Co-op will face, commitment and humanity have been at the heart of the Co-op. We feel that the true sense of the word 'co-operative' came to life in the Red Herring Workers' Co-op.

Our 'compañeros de trabajo y alma' (work and soul colleagues) are constantly with us in our thoughts and clearly show that age, colour and sex are irrelevant to friendship and comradeship. We are spiritually and eternally tied to them. We learnt so much from them and thank them everyday for their warmth and support.

Solidaridad, Paz y Salud'

Maria Figueroa & Victor Fenick

Sweets and Puddings

A wonderful meal is one which ends with a pudding that can simply not be refused. But so often this finale is lost as attention is focused on the preceding courses.

Sweets should be chosen to complement the rest of the meal. A light main course should give way to a sumptuous treat, whereas a simple and refreshing sweet is ideal after a rich main meal.

The following selection of recipes contains sweets and puddings which make the perfect conclusion to any meal. There is traditional toffee pudding for cold winter evenings, chocolate and fresh fruit cheesecake for a summer buffet and wicked chocolate, rum and orange mousse, a dinner party favourite.

Jo putting the finishing touches to a cheesecake.

Baklava
Sticky-sweet layers of flaky filo pastry, nuts and fruit.

Cranachan
Whisky, cream, strawberries, chocolate and nuts: who says Scotland isn't decadent?

Apple, Almond, Date and Cyder Strudel
Rich fruity flavours enveloped in filo pastry.

Chocolate and Fresh Fruit Cheesecake
Fresh and creamy, with the contrasting textures and flavours of rich chocolate and fruit.

Hazelnut and Apple Crumble Pie
Hazelnuts and Bramley apples make a quintessentially English combination, with the sweet surprise of marzipan.

Pear and Almond Tart
A sweet pastry flan filled with pears, almonds and cream cheese.

Wicked Chocolate, Rum and Orange Mousse
Rich and chocolatey, perfect for special occasions.

Chestnut and Chocolate Pudding
Deeply rich and creamy, to satisfy all your festive desires.

Traditional Toffee Pudding
A sticky loaf, wonderful served with walnut and brandy sauce.

Summer Pudding
A simple classic presentation of fresh berries captures the taste of summer.

Baklava
with chopped nut and cinnamon filling

serves 4-6

vegan

contains nuts

filling:
450g	nuts, e.g. walnuts, almonds, pistachios (coarsely chopped)
50g	brown sugar
2 tsp	ground cinnamon

syrup:
350g	brown sugar
225 ml	water
	juice of 1 lemon
1 tbsp	orange blossom water or rosewater
1	packet filo pastry
225g	margarine

To make the filling, combine the ingredients and mix well.

To make the syrup, dissolve the sugar in the water and lemon juice. Bring the mix to the boil and simmer for 10-15 minutes until it reaches the consistency of a syrup. Then add the orange blossom water (or the rosewater) and take off the heat and allow to cool.

Take a large, not too deep, baking tin (30 x 40 cm) and brush it with the melted margarine.

Take half the sheets of filo and line the tin with them, brushing each sheet with margarine.

Spread the chopped nut and cinnamon filling over the filo pastry, then cover with the remaining sheets of filo, brushing them with margarine as each one is layered.

With a sharp knife cut through all the layers diagonally to form diamond shapes.

Bake at gas mark 5 for 20-25 minutes and then at gas mark 7 for 10-15 minutes until the pastry is nicely browned.

Remove from the oven and immediately pour the chilled syrup over the baklava. Allow to cool before serving.

Cranachan

serves 4-5

contains nuts

450g	strawberries (cut into quarters)
75g	hazelnuts (toasted and coarsely chopped)
100g	plain chocolate (coarsely chopped)
275 ml	whipping cream
1 tbsp	whisky
1 tbsp	icing sugar
	grated chocolate to garnish

Combine chopped nuts and chopped chocolate.

Whip the cream until almost stiff, then add the whisky and icing sugar. Whip for a few more seconds until firm.

To assemble, take a large glass and layer the mixture as follows: strawberry, chocolate and nuts, whisky cream, strawberry, chocolate and nuts, whisky cream. Sprinkle grated chocolate on top.

Apple, Almond, Date and Cyder Strudel

serves 4-5

vegan

contains nuts

5 sheets	filo pastry
450g	cooking apples (peeled, cored and sliced)
4 tbsp	cyder
100g	dried pitted dates (chopped)
	zest and juice of 1 orange
75g	almonds (blanched, toasted and roughly chopped)
50g	margarine (melted)
2-3 tbsp	flaked almonds to decorate

Put apple, cyder, dates, orange zest and juice in a pan, cover and cook for 5 minutes until the apples are soft but not too mushy. Add the toasted, chopped almonds and leave to cool.

Take 4 sheets of filo pastry and layer them on top of each other, brushing each one with melted margarine.

Place the filling on the filo pastry and roll into a large cigar shaped parcel. The technique is exactly the same as with small filo pastry cigars.

Brush the remaining sheet of filo pastry with melted margarine and scrunch it up to resemble crumpled paper. Brush the top of the strudel with margarine and stick the sheet of crumpled filo on top. Sprinkle with the flaked almonds.

Bake at gas mark 4 for 20 minutes until golden brown.

Serve hot or cold, in slices. This dessert is naturally sweetened by the dates and has no added sugar.

Sticky Banana and Date Filo Pie

serves 6

vegan

contains nuts

50g	*margarine*
8-10	*sheets filo pastry*
6	*bananas (sliced)*
50g	*dried pitted dates (chopped)*
5 tbsp	*maple syrup*
2 tbsp	*rum*
50g	*flaked almonds*
	zest from 1 orange

Mix the bananas, dates, syrup, rum, almonds and orange zest. Stir well so bananas are well coated in liquid.

Melt the margarine and grease a 25 cm flan dish.

Take 1 sheet of filo pastry and line the dish – do not remove the excess pastry. Brush the filo with margarine and top with another layer of filo. Ensure that each sheet of filo is alternated to form a cross, ie. 1 sheet placed vertically, the next horizontally, so that there is excess filo right around the outside of the dish.

Once all the sheets of filo are lining the base of the dish pour in the banana mix.

One sheet at a time, fold in the excess filo pastry, brush with oil and repeat for the next sheet. Once all the excess filo has been folded back into the centre of the dish all the banana mix should be covered in layers of filo.

Brush the top with the remaining margarine then bake at gas mark 3 for 25-30 minutes until the filo pastry is golden brown.

Chocolate and Fresh Fruit Cheesecake serves 8-10

contains nuts

base:
100g	*digestive biscuits (crushed)*
125g	*chocolate (melted)*
50g	*hazelnuts (roasted and chopped)*

filling:
250g	*fromage frais*
600 ml	*whipping cream*
35g	*soft brown sugar*
150g	*soft fresh fruit, such as strawberries or pitted cherries*

garnish:
	chocolate for curls or
50g	*more fresh fruit*

Stir the digestive biscuits and nuts into the melted chocolate. Press into a 330 mm flan dish and chill.

Whip the cream and set aside. Blend the cheese with the sugar and fold the whipped cream into it. Gently fold the fruit into the mixture. Spoon it into the base and smooth it flat.

Decorate with more fruit or chocolate curls, made using a vegetable peeler. Chill for at least 2 hours to set before serving.

Marbled Cheesecake

Puree the fruit and swirl it gently through the cheese and cream filling for a marbled effect or use jam.

Mocha Rum Cheesecake

Omit the fruit and add 125g melted chocolate to the cream and cheese with 2 tbsp instant coffee dissolved in 3 tbsp rum. Decorate with a dusting of cocoa powder.

Cranberry Cheesecake

Omit the fruit in the filling. Instead, when well set, cover the top with 250g of sweet cranberry sauce.

Hazelnut and Apple Crumble Pie

serves 8

vegan

contains nuts

crust:

375g	*wholemeal flour*
175g	*roasted ground hazelnuts*
125g	*unrefined soft brown sugar*
2½ tsp	*cinnamon*
200g	*margarine*
2 tsp	*vanilla essence*
1 tbsp	*soya milk*

filling:

120g	*thinly sliced marzipan*
5	*large Bramley apples*
125g	*sultanas*
6 tbsp	*water*
2 tbsp	*wholemeal flour*
125g	*sugar*

Combine all the crust ingredients and press ½ into a 330 mm pie dish to cover the bottom and sides.

Line the base with slices of marzipan.

Put the apples, sultanas and water into a wide-based pan in a thin layer. Cook on a low heat for 5 minutes until just tender. Remove from the heat and add flour and sugar.

Put the apple mixture into the pastry shell on top of the marzipan. Crumble the remaining pastry over to cover apples.

Bake at gas mark 5 for 30 minutes until golden brown.

Cool and serve.

Pear and Almond Tart

serves 6

contains nuts

base:
75g	85% flour
75g	fine maizemeal
50g	medium cornmeal
75g	brown sugar
1	egg (beaten)
100g	margarine

filling:
100g	ground almonds
50g	brown sugar
200g	cream cheese
3 drops	almond essence
3-4	conference pears (peeled and sliced lengthways)
	juice of 1 lemon

To make the base, combine flour, maizemeal and cornmeal and sugar. Rub in the margarine and mix in the egg to bind the ingredients. Press into a greased flan tin.

To make the filling, mix the sliced pears with the lemon juice. Remove the pears from the lemon juice, keeping the juice, and arrange the pear slices on the flan base.

Mix the almonds, sugar, cream cheese and almond essence with the lemon juice. Spread evenly over the pears.

Bake at gas mark 5 for about 30 minutes, until the tart is set and slightly browned.

Serve either hot or cold.

Wicked Chocolate, Rum and Orange Mousse

serves 4-6

4	eggs (separated)
200g	dark chocolate (broken into cubes)
250 ml	double cream
2 tbsp	rum
	juice and zest from 1 orange

Put the chocolate in a heatproof bowl and place over a pan of boiling water. Keep the water simmering until the chocolate has melted.

Remove the chocolate from the heat and beat in the rum, egg yolks, orange juice and orange zest.

Whisk the egg whites to form stiff peaks.

Whisk the cream until stiff.

Fold in the cream and then the egg whites.

Chill until firm.

Chestnut and Chocolate Pudding

serves 4-6
contains nuts

125g	plain chocolate
90g	margarine
120 ml	single cream
90g	caster sugar
420g	chestnut puree (bought ready made)
3	Nice biscuits
1 tbsp	brandy
50g	hazelnuts (toasted and finely chopped)

Line a 450g loaf tin with foil and brush with oil.

Melt the chocolate with the butter, cream and sugar.

Put the chestnut puree into a bowl and beat the chocolate mix into it.

Crumble the biscuits and sprinkle the brandy onto them.

Spread ⅓ of the chocolate mix on the base of the tin, then sprinkle ½ the biscuits on top. Add another ⅓ of chocolate mix, then the remaining biscuits and finally the rest of the chocolate mix.

Chill the pudding overnight.

Loosen the edges with a palette knife and turn out onto a plate. Sprinkle with the toasted chopped nuts and serve in slices.

Traditional Toffee Pudding

serves 4-6

250g	pitted dates
315 ml	boiling water
175g	brown sugar
175g	margarine
1	egg (beaten)
225g	white self-raising flour
½ tsp	bicarbonate of soda

Place the dates and boiling water in a bowl and leave to stand, so that the dates soften.

Cream the sugar and margarine until light and fluffy, then add the beaten egg.

Line 2 500g loaf tins with lightly oiled greaseproof paper.

Blend the dates and water to form a paste and add this to the sugar, margarine and egg.

Fold in the flour and bicarbonate of soda, then pour the mixture into the tins and cover with greased foil.

Bake at gas mark 5 for 50-60 minutes, checking after 45 minutes. The puddings are cooked when a skewer can be pushed into the centre and pulled out clean. Allow to cool before turning out of the tins.

Slice the puddings once they have cooled. They can be reheated easily and are delicious served with walnut and brandy sauce.

Walnut and brandy sauce

contains nuts

25g	margarine
5 tbsp	cream
5 tbsp	brown sugar
50g	walnuts (chopped)
275 ml	milk
2 tbsp	brandy

Melt the margarine and add the cream, sugar and walnuts. Cook until boiling, then gradually add the milk, stirring all the time.

Return to the boil, then remove from the heat, allow to cool slightly and add the brandy.

Summer Pudding

serves 4-6

vegan

500g	*black or red currants*
3-4 tbsp	*maple syrup*
125g	*raspberries*
125g	*strawberries*
8	*slices wholewheat bread (crusts removed)*

Put the currants and syrup in a pan and cook gently for 10-15 minutes until tender.

Add the raspberries and strawberries and leave to cook, then strain the fruit, reserving the juice.

Cut 3 circles of bread to fit the base, middle and top of a 900 ml pudding basin. Shape the remaining bread round the side of the basin and soak it with the reserved juice.

Place the base circle of bread in the basin and pour in half the fruit mixture. Top with the middle bread circle and pour in the remaining fruit. Top with the last bread circle and fold over any bread protuding from the basin.

Cover with a saucer small enough to fit inside the basin, resting on the bread and put a 500g weight on top. Leave in the fridge overnight.

To serve, loosen the bread from the side of the bowl with a palette knife and turn out onto a serving plate. Pour any remaining juice over the pudding.

Bread not Bombs

To make even a small idea a reality against all odds is an act of hope and defiance. I wanted to bring together what I believed and how I lived my life. I chose to make a modest, honest living from baking.

Through taxation we give part of our personal wages for the social betterment of all. When tax is spent on armaments we must appeal to our consciences for wars are all the same: a lot of poor people die awful deaths in order to determine who controls areas of land and resources. I decided that if I ever made a profit I would only pay tax after the Inland Revenue assured me it would not be used for armaments.

This philosophy sustained me in the face of the van breaking down, the fire grate collapsing, exhaustion, and quite real doubts about the value or sanity of continuing. It made me realise how hard others work to survive, making things in their homes to sell in uncertain markets, the world over. Endless millions struggle at the economic margins for survival. 'Bread not Bombs' is a bold demand of bread for all, not weapons for the minority to control the rest of us.

Before the Co-op was formed, as a self-employed person I had to submit my own tax returns. In the 1987/88 tax year I owed £155.25. I requested the assurance that none of my tax would be used for military expenditure. I felt that withholding this might be my only opportunity for an important symbolic gesture. At my final court case I took a barrow of bread buns as payment for my tax bill: Bread not Bombs.

Prison is a strange place but it is surprising how quickly you can get used to it. I got on very well with some of the inmates and many of them extended their friendship, showing me the ropes. I don't regret it. I learnt an awful lot. It reinforced my views on prison and punishment, starkly revealing the class nature of British society. I was asked to work in the prison bakery, a privilege as I was in for such a short sentence. Otherwise I would have been in my cell alone with my slop bucket for 23 hours a day.

The Red Herring was very supportive and also works in other ways to improve the world. We helped develop the organic, environmentally friendly, co-operative Green Man Bakery at the Earth Balance Centre in Northumberland, and hope to develop a similar commercial bakery with special needs groups at the Rising Sun farm in Wallsend. We have a long standing relationship with the Watermill, organic flour producers in Cumbria. In the long term we'd like to use only organic produce, and to have an active role in developing both the demand for and supply of organic produce. All this within the context of co-operative working and sharing skills, responsibilities and the rewards of endeavour. *Nigel Wild*

Cakes

Cakes at the Red Herring are a popular product of our bakery. We are always trying new lines, although several are still being made a decade on, remaining favourites with customers and staff!

We always have at least one vegan option on sale. Additionally we can provide cakes for birthdays, weddings and other events. Special dietary requirements can be met. The Red Herring Christmas cakes have been a great success over the years, so order well in advance, or make your own.

Ingredients and tips

As might be expected, the better the ingredients the better the end product will be. As cakes are generally a treat, why not spoil yourself and use the best ingredients you can get.

Flour: All our cakes are made with organic flour from The Watermill in Cumbria. You can use 85% or unbleached white flour or a combination of the two. Self-raising flour can be used if you reduce or eliminate the baking powder.

Eggs: We always use free range eggs in all our produce.

Margarine: We use Suma Sunflower margarine but butter can be used for all the recipes.

Sugar: We use unrefined soft brown sugar.

Baking powder: We make our own from a combination of two thirds cream of tartar and one third bicarbonate of soda.

Keep your ingredients at room temperature. Melted or extremely soft margarine will alter the texture of a cooked cake.

Cooking times are all approximate and can vary from oven to oven. Equally good results will be achieved whether you use a gas oven or an electric one. Try and avoid checking a cake until it is nearly cooked, as the rush of cold air could make it sink.

To check whether your cake is cooked gently push a skewer into the thickest part of the cake and withdraw it slowly. If it comes out clean leave your cake to cool, if it is coated with uncooked mix, return the cake to the oven for further cooking.

As a general rule keep wet and dry ingredients separate and bake them as soon as they are mixed. If you leave a wet cake mixture for too long it will deactivate the baking powder and the cake will not rise.

Apricot Crumble Cake
Belly timber with a hint of French tart and nuts.

Carrot cake
Moist sweet comfort

Sticky Lemon Cake
Simple, succulent, delicious.

Banana and Walnut Cake
A nutty Red Herring vegan classic.

Chocolate, Orange and Brandy Cake
Rich and right.

Rocca Cake
Rum and moccha chocolate.

Chocolate and Greek Yoghurt Cake
Chocolate and yoghurt topping to a moist cake – a lovely combination.

Anna Cake
Lumps of chocolate in a rum-enhanced sponge.

Chocolate Biscuit Cake
Melt and fridge, quick and lush.

Cherry and Almond Cake
A very rich nutty flapjack; a longstanding vegan favourite.

Nichole in the shop: let them eat cake.

Apricot Crumble Cake

serves 8

crumble:

115g	*85% flour*
½ tsp	*baking powder*
85g	*sugar*
85g	*margarine*

cake:

170g	*85% flour*
1 tsp	*baking powder*
	pinch of salt
85g	*sugar*
85g	*margarine*
2	*eggs (for a vegan alternative use 2 tbsp soya flour mixed to a paste with water)*
3 tbsp	*milk or soya milk*

filling:

170g	*apricots*

topping:

1 tbsp	*cinnamon*
1 tbsp	*sugar*

Prepare the filling by putting the apricots into a pan with just enough water to cover them and simmering until pulpy. Keep checking they have enough water.

Prepare the crumble mixture. Rub the flour, baking powder and margarine together until crumbly. Stir in the sugar then sprinkle in a dessert spoon of water and mix with a fork until coarse and lumpy.

Prepare the cake mixture. Place the flour, salt, margarine, sugar, egg (or soya paste), essence and milk (or soya milk) together in a bowl. Beat for a couple of minutes, then spread evenly in the base of a greased 250 mm round cake tin.

Cover the cake mixture with the apricots.

Sprinkle the crumble topping over the apricots.

Bake at gas mark 4 in the centre of the oven for about 1 hour.

Leave to cool, then sprinkle with the cinnamon and sugar.

Carrot Cake

serves 8

225g	sugar
175 ml	sunflower oil
3	eggs
225g	85% flour
225g	carrots (grated)
115g	sultanas
1/5 tsp	vanilla essence
1 tsp	cinnamon
½ tsp	ginger
½ tsp	salt
1 tsp	baking powder

Beat the oil, sugar and eggs together until well mixed.

Fold in the rest of the ingredients.

Pour into a greased 250 mm round cake tin.

Bake at gas mark 4 for about 45 minutes to 1 hour.

Sticky Lemon Cake

serves 8

225g	margarine
225g	sugar
3	eggs
225g	85% flour
1 tsp	baking powder
	zest from 2 lemons
syrup topping:	
	juice from 2 lemons
55g	sugar

Cream the margarine and sugar until light and fluffy, then add the eggs and beat well. Add the zest of the lemons.

Fold in the flour and baking powder.

Put into a greased 250 mm round cake tin and bake at gas mark 4 for about 45 minutes.

Heat the syrup and lemon juice in a bowl over a pan of boiling water until the sugar is dissolved.

Prick the cooked cake all over with a fork and spoon the syrup mixture evenly over the top.

Banana and Walnut Cake

serves 8
vegan
contains nuts

115g	*sugar*
170g	*margarine*
225g	*85% flour*
170g	*walnuts*
2 tsp	*soya flour*
3	*bananas (the riper the better)*
1 tsp	*baking powder*
topping:	
100g	*vegan chocolate*
25g	*margarine*

Cream the margarine and sugar until light and fluffy.

Add the whole bananas and mix well until the bananas are broken up and evenly distributed.

Make a paste with the soya flour and a little water and fold in this and the rest of the ingredients except the chocolate and remaining margarine.

Pour into a greased 250 mm round cake tin and bake at gas mark 4 for 30 minutes.

When the cake is cooked and has cooled, melt the margarine and chocolate together in a bowl over a pan of boiling water and spread over the top of the cake.

An egg can be substituted for the soya flour if you are not vegan.

Chocolate, Orange and Brandy Cake serves 8

225g	*margarine*
225g	*sugar*
3	*eggs*
225g	*85% flour*
1 tsp	*baking powder*
1 tbsp	*cocoa powder (sieved)*
225g	*Bournville chocolate (chopped)*
	zest of 2 oranges
syrup:	*juice of 2 oranges*
5g	*sugar*
1 tbsp	*brandy*

Cream the margarine and sugar until light and fluffy. Add the eggs and beat well. Add the orange zest.

Fold in the flour, cocoa and baking powder.

Pour into a greased 250 mm round cake tin and sprinkle with chopped chocolate.

Bake at gas mark 4 for about 40 minutes.

Heat the orange juice and sugar in a bowl over a pan of boiling water until the sugar is dissolved to make a syrup. Add the brandy and spoon evenly over the cooked cake.

Rocca Cake serves 8

225g	*margarine*
225g	*sugar*
3	*eggs*
225g	*flour*
1 tsp	*baking powder*
1 tbsp	*instant coffee*
225g	*Bournville chocolate (grated or chopped)*
1 tbsp	*rum*

Mix the coffee with a little boiling water to make a paste and leave to cool.

Cream the margarine and sugar until light and fluffy, then beat in the eggs. Mix in the coffee paste.

Fold in all the other ingredients (except the chocolate and the rum).

Put into a greased 250 mm round cake tin and then sprinkle the chocolate over the cake mix.

Bake at gas mark 4 for about 45 minutes.

When cool, sprinkle with the rum.

Chocolate and Greek Yoghurt Cake serves 8

225g	margarine
225g	sugar
3	eggs
50 ml	milk
225g	85% flour
1 tbsp	cocoa powder (sieved)
1 tsp	baking powder
topping:	
100g	Bournville chocolate
100g	Greek yoghurt

Cream the margarine and sugar until light and fluffy, then add the eggs and beat well.

Fold in the remaining ingredients (except the chocolate and yoghurt).

Put into a greased 250 mm round cake tin and bake at gas mark 3 for about 30-40 minutes.

Make the topping by melting the Bournville chocolate over a pan of boiling water. Once melted stir in the yoghurt and mix well.

Allow the topping and cake to cool a little, then spread the topping over the cake.

Anna Cake

serves 6-8

Rum and chocolate chip

contains nuts

225g	margarine
225g	sugar
3	eggs
170g	85% flour
55g	ground almonds
1 tsp	baking powder
25g	mixed peel
1/5 tsp	vanilla essence
225g	Bournville chocolate
1 tbsp	rum

Cream the margarine and sugar until light and fluffy, then add the eggs and beat well.

Fold in the other ingredients, except the chocolate and rum.

Pour into a greased 250 mm round cake tin and sprinkle with chopped chocolate.

Bake at gas mark 4 for about 30 minutes.

Once cooked and cool, sprinkle with the rum.

Chocolate Biscuit Cake

serves 6-8

vegan

This is a very quick and easy cake. It does not require cooking and if made with oatcakes rather than digestives it is gluten free.

115g	sugar
115g	margarine
335g	vegan chocolate
170g	glace cherries
170g	currants
85g	porridge oats
450g	oatcakes or digestive biscuits

Melt the margarine and half the chocolate in a pan over a low heat. Then mix in the sugar and fruit and stir well.

Crumble biscuits or oatcakes until coarsely ground. Mix into the fruit and melted chocolate.

Line and grease 2 baking trays and spread the mixture evenly over these.

Melt the remaining chocolate in a bowl over a pan of boiling water and spread the melted chocolate over the cake.

Chill in the refrigerator until set.

Cherry and Almond Cake

serves 8-10

vegan

contains nuts

225g	*margarine*
225g	*soft brown sugar*
175g	*85% flour*
125g	*porridge oats*
175g	*ground almonds*
225g	*undyed cherries*
50g	*flaked almonds*

Cream sugar and margarine. Add the other ingredients, except the flaked almonds, and mix thoroughly.

Press into a greased 250mm round cake tin and sprinkle the flaked almonds on top, pushing them into the dough slightly.

Bake at gas mark 4 for about 30 minutes.

Love, Pure Love

'It never fails to amaze me how many misconceptions arise from the seemingly innocent term 'Workers Co-operative'. These range from the business being a front for some extremist political organisation whose sole aim is to overthrow the government (if only!) to us being a bunch of students running a cafe between lectures (as if!).

I remember one evening when a man approached the counter to order. From his seriously sharp three-piece pinstripe suit, immaculate coiffure and mobile phone dangling ostentatiously from his hand it was clear he was not your regular 'Red Herring' customer. I was struck by his condescending manner and air of bemused curiosity as he surveyed our humble establishment.

When he returned to settle his bill – 'No, I'm sorry but we don't accept American Express' – his curiosity had got the better of him and he asked me: 'What's with this workers' co-operative?'

I proceeded to explain our modus operandi and its underlying philosophy, but I got the impression that he was not really listening. 'Are you a profit-making organisation then?' he inquired aggressively.

'Yes, we made a small profit last year', I replied, growing irritated.

Then, with an arrogant flourish and a tone as if to say, get out of this one if you can, he asked: 'So what brings you to work each morning?'

I was tempted to reply 'the bus', but I fixed him with my best beatific smile and said, with heart-rending sincerity, 'Love, pure love'.

This stopped him dead. He stared hard at me, trying to work out if I was for real, but all he received in return was this radiant smile. He turned on his heel and beat a hasty retreat in a state of befuddlement. Once he was safely out of the door the kitchen erupted in laughter.

I think that there was more than a grain of truth in my facetious answer to our visitor from the world of cut-throat capitalism. I have certainly never known harder work, yet I have never found work more rewarding. I know that the love and friendships forged in the heat of that kitchen will endure as, I hope, will the Red Herring. Throughout the dark years of Thatcherism and the blind, heartless dogma of market economics, how reassuring to witness the continued survival of a small business run on sound egalitarian principles. I am sure that with the love and dedication of the Red Herring workers and the loyalty of its appreciative customers it will continue to flourish.'

Simon Shields

'Bake to Basics': The Red Herring as a Workers' Co-operative

'The ideals of the co-operative movement embrace equality, democracy, mutual self help and economic and social justice . . . Co-operatives develop people's ability to participate in society. They not only provide jobs and an income for those who work for them but also give a real training in the democratic practices necessary for the proper running of our society . . . Co-operation in common productive endeavour helps people achieve their full potential.'
ICOM President John Smith MP, QC, November 1993

The term 'Workers' Co-operative' is frequently misunderstood, its significance overlooked and effectiveness as a business structure underestimated. This section is aimed at putting the record straight, providing information about the Co-operative Movement both in historical terms and its relevance to the present economic climate.

A small fish in a big sea

In 1844 a band of cloggers, tailors and weavers set up a tiny store in Rochdale, Lancashire, with an idea that was to grow into the modern Co-operative Movement. Today co-operative businesses in the UK have a combined turnover of £10 billion and employ more than 140,000 people. Worldwide there are organisations in more than 100 countries belonging to the International Co-operative Alliance with a total membership of 700 million. The Red Herring is really a very small fish in an enormous sea!

What defines a co-operative business?

The Red Herring in practice shares many of the characteristics of other small businesses, but exhibits some special features which differentiate it from conventional management. We are registered under the Companies Act and all nine members are directors, therefore the risks, responsibilities and rewards are shared considerations. The business is controlled democratically putting into practice the principles of social justice and equal opportunities.

All the members of the Red Herring Co-operative attend meetings once every three weeks. These are minuted, chaired and follow an agenda which has been compiled during the previous week. The issues can include matters concerning the everyday running of the business, as well as more long term aims of the Co-operative. Although the official line is 'one member, one vote' consensus is usually achieved through discussion, rather than casting individual votes. Larger co-ops usually

elect a representative committee, who are responsible for decision-making and general management of the business.

Learning to swim at the Red Herring

For the success of any enterprise it is essential to have staff who are interested, competent, self-confident and well informed on all aspects of the company. Full business training and excellent internal communications are an absolute requisite for any company, the only difference being that co-operatives assume that requirement from the outset.

Therefore, the Red Herring has strongly focused upon developing in-house training as a priority, exchanging the skills and experience which have evolved over the last decade. In addition members are always bringing new ideas and input which often challenge the existing systems. This openness to transition and change within the business can be refreshing and avoids the everyday often monotonous jobs becoming inefficient or stagnant.

Collective decision-making

Co-operatives are open to decide on their own wage distribution, either adopting an equal or differential pay structure which may be dictated by various factors, for example length of service, social need, experience. The Red Herring Co-op members all receive the same pay.

Because the Red Herring is owned and controlled by the people who work there, the members are free to decide how they will apply any profits made. The dedicated commitment and pioneering ground contributed by the original workforce has firmly established the foundations of a thriving business. This stability has provided an environment conducive to our slow yet steady development.

In 1992 we were able to refurnish the cafe – when regular customers started to bring screwdrivers in to mend the chairs they were deemed unsafe for the daily stress of customer use. In terms of kitchen and bakery equipment investments were made as well. An industrial vegetable preparation machine affectionately known as 'Robocop', and just last year, a dough mixer which, being three times the size of our previous one, often leaves us wondering how we managed prior to its arrival.

Ethical code of practice

The Red Herring attempts to combine commercial aims with social aims, to provide fairer and more human working conditions. Our external and internal business relationships are ruled by the logic of mutual benefit rather than that of exploitation. We look to support other co-operatives and local businesses within the community.

We have an active environmental policy, recycling, composting and minimising waste where ever possible.

We also prioritise fair traded produce. As a Co-operative we reject any discrimination for sexual, social, racial, political or religious reasons, holding a firm commitment to treating every individual equally.

Promoting co-ops within the community

The Red Herring has spent several years participating and often instigating programmes to promote the co-operative ethos within the community. These have included training, work placements, stalls and educational events with schools. All of these give practical learning through a co-operative example. We endeavour to continue this involvement and to develop further such projects.

We have recently finished a number of training sessions with the Greenman Bakery Co-op, who are based at the Earth Balance centre in Ashington. These included advice on both a structured and informal basis concerning co-operative management and practical bakery skills.

Additionally, we have run several work placements with students qualifying in Careers Guidance and young people in their final year of secondary school. We have been involved in annual school events, doing oven building and bread making with younger children. Occasionally we have done food stalls at local festivals including ones organised by the Tyne and Wear Anti-Fascist group and the May Day Committee.

We endeavour to support local artists by exhibiting their work on a monthly rotational basis. There is also space allocated in the cafe for posters advertising exhibitions, local events and accommodation.

Future aims

We are committed to building upon the work that people have contributed to the Co-op during the past decade. To continue developing the business in terms of our service and diversity. Therefore, improving the welfare and conditions of our workforce, whilst also acknowledging the loyalty of many of our customers who have supported us for several years. This insight into co-operative working is intended to inform and hopefully will even inspire!

Jenny Jones

Someone to Catch You

'One Tuesday morning I arrived at the bakery to start a shift with Nigel, my co-worker that week. We started on our usual banter exchanging tales of our weekend's happenings. Nigel soon embarked on an account of a rather gruesome accident involving his partner Louise, who had fallen on a knife whilst harvesting cauliflowers from their allotment. The injury had been rather nasty and painful, the knife having gone into her back right up to the hilt; the wound although potentially very damaging was fortunately of no serious consequence.

Whilst he recounted the incident, in graphic detail, I was suddenly overcome with a nauseous and dizzy sensation. Nigel, noticing my eyes glazing over, moved towards me just in time to catch me before hitting the concrete bakery floor. For the first time in my life I had fainted.

I regained consciousness a couple of seconds later, to see a concerned and worried looking Nigel; once he saw I was alright he passed me some Bournville and carried on baking. I lay on the floor a few minutes longer, listening to the strangely comforting whirr of the dough mixing machine and eating the chocolate. Soon I felt fine and continued with the rest of my shift.

A few days later I came across a card entitled 'There is always someone to catch you when you fall', which I gave to Nigel. Although it referred to this one incident, in many ways it summarises the overwhelming support myself and many others have felt working at the Red Herring. Not only has there 'always been someone to catch you when you fall', but also so many different directions in which you can climb.'
Jenny Jones

An empty kitchen awaiting another shift, another cycle of cooking, consuming and cleaning.

Index

[V] indicates that the recipe is vegan.